Down and Dirty ...

ANDREA FRAZER

Down and Dirty in the Dordogne

ISBN: 9798366140317

This edition is published by JDI Publications 2022

Copyright © 2014 by Andrea Frazer

The right of Andrea Frazer to be identified as the Author of the Work has been asserted by her in accordance with the Copyright, Designs and Patents Act, 1988

All rights reserved.

No part of this publication can be reproduced, stored or transmitted in any form or by any means, electronic or mechanical, without the prior permission in writing from the publishers.

TABLE OF CONTENTS

PROLOGUE: How it happened
CHAPTER ONE:
The search begins; Deaf estate agents and ghosts; Our hearts are lost; Tragedy and disharmony; Surprise decision, surprise chateau, and surprise teabags; What price loyalty? We decide to flee.
CHAPTER TWO:
OMG!; Meeting the neighbours; First Wood Delivery; Bringing home the cats; No hot water and no power supply for the cooker; First visitors
CHAPTER THREE:
White goods and white weather; Taming the garden and the trouble with bonfires; Joining a choral society
CHAPTER FOUR:
Tracteur and *motobineuse*; Joining the Monday quintet; Stopping the back wall from falling off the house; Meeting the builders
CHAPTER FIVE:
Old friends again; A run-in with the natives; Let the planting begin, New friends; Some pitfalls in learning the lingo; Disaster; Marbles meets his first chicken
CHAPTER SIX:
Lizards and other pests; Monkey does VE Day; Lucy; Francis and partner
CHAPTER SEVEN:
Cats and coypu; *Espèce de vache*!; Tragedy; UK – pronounced yuk; Coming back home; The baby grand; The scales of justice are rebalanced
CHAPTER EIGHT:
This house eats furniture; Judith Iscariot does not live in this vicinity; Snakes; Our first harvest oh help!, Let the Refurbishment begin; *Cornichon* – or gherkins, to you; Tomatoes; A gluttony of gluts; Dwarves and henges; A bit

of a do – French style
CHAPTER NINE:
The Joys of jamming; The joys of musical jamming; Downhill all the way
CHAPTER TEN:
Friday is bankruptcy day; A lovely visit from family; The dark shadow of illness; An encounter with a really low blood sugar level; The first attempt on my life in a French hospital, Front door blues
CHAPTER ELEVEN:
Lost in France; The Outlaws have a stab at seeing me off; The hospital makes a second attempt on my life
CHAPTER TWELVE:
Television; The opening of a new library; More wood already; The great chutney disaster of 2008; Never believe anybody when it comes to insurance
CHAPTER THIRTEEN:
We just can't afford the staff, these days; A very English carol party; Singing in the Abbey; In the bleak midwinter; First Christmas without a crowd; Long John Turkey; Looking to the future
CHAPTER FOURTEEN:
First tragedy of the year; an unfortunate incident; I am a raspberry; a cavalcade of cats
CHAPTER FIFTEEN:
Clay and concrete; back in the hamster wheel again; the smothering coils of bureaucracy; enter an old friend; even more cats

Author's note: After the momentous decision, we realised we would be heading down to the Dordogne, but we never realised how filthy and dirty we would get: dust, cobwebs, paint, wood treatments, soil and general grime – we wore them all as a symbol of what we were attempting.

PROLOGUE

HOW IT HAPPENED

Life had become somewhat boring. Only Harry, our younger son out of four children, remained at home, and he worked full-time. Ian, my husband, was out of the house all day, too. I had previously been teaching Greek at two colleges, but they were both about twenty-five miles away, and I tired of the driving for what, in reality, was only a very small number of hours work. I still taught music at home, but that occupied very little of my time.

The house was absolutely immaculate (!) and I had a routine for each day's cleaning. We had moved into the house, with five bedrooms and a double garage – yummy! – when it was brand new a few years ago, and there was simply nothing to do once we had landscaped the garden and put in an above-ground pool. Life felt empty. This was *not* me. There was no challenge in my life: it was simply too easy. Well, that was like a red rag to a bull for the gods of fate, and, very soon, life would be nothing like easy, but full of challenges I never thought I would have to face.

We had started our married life in Sussex in a tiny flat only two miles from where I had lived all my life. After about a year we had weathered getting a mortgage, where begging was very much the order of the day, and a woman's salary was sneered at when making calculations of eligibility, and had taken the momentous decision, for me, to move seven miles down the coast to the next town to buy our first house. We went on to buy two further houses in that town and spent in total twenty-four years there bringing up four children.

We were very much in a rut and would have stayed that way if Ian had not declared one day that he was not going to look for his next job based on where we lived but was going to look for a job he wanted and relocate if necessary. Well this was a bombshell. I had barely got over moving seven miles from where I was born! Subsequently, he got a job one hundred miles away and we moved to Wiltshire, a major event for me but one we didn't regret.

Now here we were in our new five-bedroomed house.

Just over a year after my mother died, Ian came home from work and said that there was a possibility that he might be able to get voluntary redundancy, and expressed his opinion that he would like, if possible, to move to France, as he had harboured hopes of doing that since his fiftieth birthday, when we had had a holiday there with friends, and had discussed with me retiring at fifty-five and doing just that.

Hold your cotton-pickin' horses, I thought, as he explained the situation to me. He was only fifty-two, and I thought I still had three years to talk him out of it. Of all the countries in the world, France was probably at the very bottom of my list for places I would like to live, just below North Korea. Don't ask me why – it just was.

I would have to get my skates on to talk him round to our original idea of retiring to Greece, something of which I believed I was perfectly capable. After all, we had been together since we were both seventeen in 1972. We had more or less grown up together, and had faced many bogies during this time. This was our third recession together and surely a little bit of wistfulness about France could be easily buried.

Ian had got three per cent in his "O" level French mock examination, and I had only done a wee bit in junior school, and only oral at that. Written French was a complete mystery to me.

Surely the world was our oyster and not our *huître*. I had spent years getting a Fellowship Diploma in Greek for our retirement and now I was being asked to give it all up for a language that sounded to me like someone being sick in a bucket.

He wasn't giving in at the first tackle, however. 'We've got that villa booked for May,' he announced with a crocodile smile. 'Why don't we do a little practice house-hunting then? My parents are coming with us, and they can give us their opinion.' I resisted the urge to reach for the arsenic – whether for me or for him I had no idea – and pointed out that we certainly couldn't afford to live in the Dordogne.

'That's okay,' he agreed, with another of his dangerous little smirks. 'At least it will give us an idea of the French property market, and what French houses are like – a sort of overall view.'

Of course, I fell for it, 'You *do* understand that this is just an *exploratory* exercise?' I asked him, as he pored over details of yet more properties.

'No problem,' he replied. 'It's just to get a feel for things.'

'And you *will* remember the list you made: must have heating, be reasonably modernised if it's old, must not need rewiring or re-plumbing. We've got to tick all the boxes, even if it *is* just an exercise,' I reminded him. 'And we must be in walking distance of a little bar/restaurant and a bakery, have lots of land, but have no direct neighbours.'

He grinned at me like the big bad wolf contemplating a roast pork dinner, and off we went, two babes, into the dark, dark woods of the French property world.

Well, May came and we flew off to France with Ian's parents, David and Brenda, to start our holiday in the Dordogne.

It certainly was a beautiful area with swathes of lush green fields and stands of trees interspersed like charms on a bracelet. We also strayed into the Double Forest, an area that had been, in days of yore, a swamp which was replanted by Napoleon III, and now was mixed woodland with charming open areas containing picture-book villages and hamlets.

At both sides of all the teeny-weeny roads were ditches, modern-day evidence of the need still to keep this land drained and, as the itsy-bitsy roads had neither cat's eyes nor white lines, I dreaded the thought of having to drive here, on the wrong side of the road, with no side-lines to keep me out of said ditches, or centre-line to keep me from straying on to the wrong side, even though there was hardly room for two sides on many of the routes.

All this was set in a slightly rolling landscape that, to me, made it appear a cross between leafy Sussex and undulating Wiltshire. How could I help not but be captivated with its natural beauty?

The larger towns, Bordeaux, Périgueux, and Angoulême, were very widely spaced, and smaller towns had the charm of the mid-twentieth century, with no department or chain stores – and the French say the English are a nation of shopkeepers! – Here they were, almost to a man – or woman – keeping some of the tiniest shops I have ever squeezed into.

When the scenery did threaten to get a bit urban, it justified itself with ancient architecture and charming ironwork balconies and gates. It was only in the shops that I found the jarring note of the French language. Maybe, but just maybe, I could live here if I either wore earplugs or saw out my existence as a hermit.

We had made all our appointments in advance, so already had a viewing schedule for the Monday, Wednesday and Friday of our week away. This was only fair, as the four of us had only hired one car, and we needed to leave it free for Ian's parents to have a say in what we did on some of the days. This turned out to be a lucky arrangement. I would like to point out that, due to David's frequent postings with the RAF, he had never been on holiday with them before, so it was a new experience for all four of us.

CHAPTER ONE

The search begins; Deaf estate agents and ghosts; Our hearts are lost; Tragedy and disharmony; Surprise decision, surprise chateau, and surprise teabags; What price loyalty? We decide to flee.

THE SEARCH BEGINS

We had made our instructions absolutely clear as to what we wanted, and set out on the Monday with high hopes. The first property we were taken to was miles away on little country roads and it became obvious that the estate agent was having difficulty finding it. Finally we arrived at the property which was positioned on a strange five-way junction and appeared to be split across it, with the house on one side and the outbuildings on the other. It was also only a couple of hundred yards from a chicken farm. Not only was the smell gut-wrenching, but the current owner foolishly told us that we would only be disturbed about once every six weeks when they slaughtered the birds. The whole place was also absolutely covered in pine-cladding, including the ceilings, and was poky, all the bedrooms having been built in the eaves from what had obviously, once upon a time, been a bungalow. While we were there the estate agent was also trying to put pressure on the vendor to lower her asking price, in hushed and hissed whispers. She needn't have wasted her time because as far as we were concerned it was a reject!

The second house sounded very interesting, and was in the woods looking down a hillside. From the outside it looked fine. Inside, the smell of fresh paint assailed our nostrils, and left us in two minds. Had the owners just decorated, or were they trying to cover up something?

The house opened up into what we identified as the kitchen. We knew it was the kitchen because there was an old stone sink balanced on piles of bricks in it. The next thing we really took notice of was the fact that it had a pool, which we were very anxious to see. How naïve we were. The pool was an above-ground one, which was quite acceptable as we already had one at home, but ours wasn't covered by a thick layer of green scum and mould, and sagging at the sides.

Brenda and I took this opportunity to use the facilities. These were the final straw. As she came down the stairs after her visit, I looked at her, she looked at me, and I drew on my minimal French to inform the estate agent that this house was horrible, and that we were leaving – now.

At the next house we were to meet the agent in what turned out to be a really beautiful little village, and our hopes soared. If the house were here, Ian would be laughing. We must have looked very happy when the agent introduced herself to us, and said that we were going to view what had been a glass-blower's house.

She got back into her car and asked us to follow her, at which point she drove out of the village and miles down the road, where she eventually stopped in a seedy little hamlet, outside a rather run-down house. Our optimism immediately evaporated.

Inside, the house was very small, and in absolute disarray with children's toys, coats and wellington boots, and enough clutter to furnish the needs of at least two jumble sales. Also, there didn't seem to be any garden. Slowly and patiently the agent explained to us that the garden was across the road, at which point she took us outside and pointed over the tarmac to a weed-choked, steep downhill run of 'garden', decorated with mounds of rubbish and a tumbledown building that might once have been a garage or a large shed. It was too dilapidated to identify which. Reject.

That was our first day's viewing, and the parents-in-law were looking very down in the mouth. The next day they said they wanted to visit Cognac, and we left them to it preferring to go through the details we had for our other two days of viewing, and assess the prospects of hitting gold, although, of course, this was only a practice-run, wasn't it?

DEAF ESTATE AGENTS AND GHOSTS

On Wednesday, we all started out again with a list of appointments, but a not so buoyant set of parents-in-law. We couldn't understand why, as we had made our intentions perfectly clear, and they had seemed enthusiastic to go along with the idea.

The stipulation that we have plenty of privacy was one of our most important criteria, and we were aghast when the agent steered us towards an old house which had a terrace of housing just a few feet across from its frontage, and children over-running the whole little dividing section. A few yards before one reached the houses there were literally dozens of abandoned cars, motorcycles, and other vehicles. It looked like a wrecking yard and had absolutely no kerb-appeal whatsoever.

We were in the agent's car this time, and we asked her what she hadn't understood about being away from other dwellings. A few more bricks and this would actually become just another part of the terrace opposite. The people there were visibly into large families – large young families! We refused to get out of the car and she had the grace to apologise.

She took us next to a house that was in a small town, and on a corner, so it had no visible land at all. We only had this explained to us after we had examined the accommodation. The ground floor was all bedrooms, although we could not work out why, as there were people walking past the windows and French doors constantly.

On the first floor was the most fabulous room we could have asked for, vast and medieval, with suitably over-sized furniture, but the kitchen was a disgrace. On asking about the land, as there was supposed to be a pool as well, the agent informed us that this was – again – across the road, which we had noticed was quite busy.

It proved to be a beautifully kept piece of land, but the really outrageous thing was that the current owners didn't want to sell the pool, and would retain that part of the garden which also contained the garage and the rear access! To add insult to injury, they also wanted to retain a strip of land from the front of the garden, including the gate, to have access to what would not be, now, the new buyers' swimming pool. Reject!

Our third viewing for the day was a house that had just been renovated. This could have been interesting but, it had an unfortunate position on the corner of a T-junction which carried quite a lot of traffic, although it did have a proper pool.

Now, the French idea of renovation is nothing like that of the English, and we entered to find that it looked like there had been a time warp, and we were back in the 1970s, in a house that had been done up by Terry and June. The only thing that was missing was glam rock playing on the radio.

All the beams had been painted white (!) and the ground floor was covered in rich red tiles. The kitchen part of this open-plan living was in pine, and the walls were also clad with it. When we managed to get a couple of private words, we decided that the only thing to do with this place would be to relocate it somewhere else, then gut it, or possibly commit arson. Reject!

We had a busy schedule that day, and were now off to a

maison de maître, defined as definitely a home of some class. I think I'd have placed it at the bottom of the class. The kitchen was through an empty room described as a dining room, and was a shed-ware horror that appeared to be situated in a not-very-roomy pantry. Although there was a huge living room, the signs of neglect were everywhere, not least in the Christmas decorations still stuck to the glass of the windows.

Upstairs, where I went on my own while Ian conversed with the agent, I found the bedrooms okay, but a further and very narrow flight of stairs led to a second floor. This was reached by a trapdoor which had been left conveniently open. I popped my head through, and was just getting the rest of my body through, when I froze. I wasn't alone. There was a palpable presence up here, and it wasn't living.

Now, I'm no psychic, nor am I gullible, but I definitely felt eyes on me, and something taking note of my every movement. I flew down the two flights of stairs and arrived, panting, in the garden where Ian and the agent were still gassing like old friends. 'What about the garden,' I asked, not wishing to discuss what had just happened, in case I was losing my marbles.

'The garden is only part of what you can see,' explained the agent, and I thought, here we go again. 'If you look down this gravel road and past the first two fields you can just see the rest of the land.' It was some 500 yards away!

What finished it for me was when a train went past, so close to the property that we could see the expressions on the passengers' faces. I invited Ian to look at the first and second floors, volunteering to stay outside, as it was such a lovely day. I simply couldn't go inside again, let alone visualise buying and living in this haunted horror. Ian, of course, felt nothing, but was so put off by the split in ownership of the land, and the bad layout of the ground floor, coupled with the amount of work there would be to do, not to mention the railway line, that we were able to label this one, too, reject!

OUR HEARTS ARE LOST

At our final appointment at the end of our arranged viewings and, incidentally, our tethers, we came across a house that I had determined we would look at when we had found it exploring the internet, before we left the shores of good old Blighty. Ian had shown no interest in it whatsoever, which only made me more adamant that we should look it over, so here we were, fifteen minutes past the time the agent was supposed to meet us, and utterly alone outside a house that looked as if it had not been cared for since the Second World War, if then.

Having spotted us hanging about suspiciously in the tiny hamlet of Saint-Sylvain, which only boasted a medieval church, a lake, and seven or eight houses, the owner (who actually didn't live there any more, and had moved away about a year ago, but had just happened to pop over today) came out to see what we were up to. With her came one of the largest dogs I have ever seen.

This looked hopeful, and we waved the property details at her. She spoke no English. That was great, because we spoke virtually no French. So, there we were, with no estate agent to verify our credentials, a non-English speaking owner who seemed not to have been informed of our arrival, barely a word of French between us (and certainly not a whole sentence) and the Hound of the Baskervilles eyeing us up as if we might provide a dainty snack for him.

The first room we were shown was the dining room. On the outside walls of this room were signs for a now-defunct restaurant and, apparently, this had been a regular haunt of the Resistance during the war, one customer actually being shot by the Germans as he tried to flee the building. Nice friendly place this must have been, back then!

The house had three large downstairs rooms, the middle one containing a kitchen sink and a plastic shower cubicle. This, with a lavatory in a nasty little cubicle under the stairs, comprised the water supply for the whole house. With mime and the odd word here and there that conveyed her meaning, the owner explained that this was the room in which, when she had been preparing to replace the fibre-board floor, she had encountered two skeletons, and a coin dating from the early 1600s.

Where had she moved them? we enquired, to the best of our ability. She hadn't. That was all right then, wasn't it? No archaeologists would come snooping round here looking for human remains. Aargh! She did show us the coin, however.

The house had two staircases (which, for some mad reason, I've always wanted): one which led to two inter-connecting bedrooms on the north side – something I'd always refused point-blank to consider when house-hunting in the past. The other, at the south end, led to a place large enough to be a barn, but with all its rooms pulled out, so that it was possible to see right up to the roof tiles, and beyond, in some places. Large areas of the floor were outlined in red paint-sprayed lines, and warned of unsafe floorboards.

The third downstairs room had a wooden floor that swayed like the deck of a ship, due to the fact that it had been installed only about four inches above the earth, as the building had no foundations, and it was rumoured that the Resistance's weapons were buried in the ground thereunder.

This was not of the remotest interest to me, however, as I had just caught sight of the wall, to the right, as one entered the room. It was *columbage*, with the most beautifully arranged thin tiles at an angle of about forty-five degrees, the beams in between, time-scarred and leaning at a charming angle that was not scary. Rather, it was enchanting, showing how long the property had stood there, and redolent of centuries of history. I was in love. There hadn't been a box to tick for that.

At that point, she produced a UFO magazine in French and, there, on the front cover, was a large black and white picture of this house, with a flying saucer hovering over it. This was priceless stuff. By the time she'd got to the story about the two kilograms of gold that were rumoured to be secreted on the property, we were hooked. This was straight out of Enid Blyton. All we needed were three friends and a dog called Timmy.

Needless to say, we ditched our soulless little list of boxes to be ticked, went with our hearts, even though it was a complete wreck with hardly any ceiling lights, and virtually no sockets, using jury-rigged connections involving a multitude of extension leads, giving only a slight impression of it having electricity at all.

Outside, as we sat in the car waiting for Ian's parents to get back from their sulk-induced walk, we watched a hare lope lazily along the road past the house, and heard the busy drilling of a couple of woodpeckers, the tympani accompaniment to the cooing of doves. All the scene really needed was for Walt Disney to pop his head round one of the trees and ask to make a film about the area, no doubt casting the coypu in the nearby small lake in major character roles.

The real joy was to hear these animals, hunted to extinction many years ago in the UK, and it was a delightful sound from the past that could not be experienced in our home country.

TRAGEDY AND DISHARMONY

We were both obviously excited at what this house had to offer but, as Ian's parents had given up in disgust, saying they had thought they were going to be viewing brand new villas and bungalows, and gone off for a walk, we kept our feelings to ourselves all the way back to our holiday accommodation.

We had got to the position now where we weren't even all eating together, as Ian's parents wouldn't touch any French foodstuff, and had refused point-blank to use the barbecue in the kitchen; so when we got back we made ourselves some enormously overstuffed baguettes, and went out on to the terrace preparatory to having a good old gossip about our last viewing.

We had barely taken a bite of our food when the mobile phone rang, and I answered it, only to find our son Harry on the other end, with the news that one of our two beautiful, brown-spotted Bengal kittens had been killed by a car, and he had found its body when he got home from work. I was heartbroken, and getting a hug out of Brenda, for comfort, was like trying to get blood out of a stone. They weren't a touchy-feely family like the one Ian and I had created. I shed many a tear that night, and missed my mother sorely.

They went out on their own again on Thursday, and refused to see any more houses. We pootled around a couple more on the Friday, but our hearts weren't in it. The death of one of the kittens that we had thought of taking to France, believing that they'd last longer than a humbug, had rattled us. Would the other one even make it to when Ian was fifty-five? And what about the house we had both fallen in love with, but failed to discuss, as we each kept it to ourselves?

The holiday villa itself had been a disappointment, consisting more of bedrooms, which we could not use, than living space, which we felt short of, there being only one living room when we could have done with two. The main reason we had booked it was because it had an indoor swimming pool, and it was only the beginning of May, so this assured us some water play. We had to pay extra for the heating of it, but that didn't matter, I packed my rubber ring, and we both looked forward to this novelty.

It turned out to be severely under-heated to the point where it was hard to stay in it for long, so chilly was the water, so Ian tracked down the cupboard where the controls were and turned the temperature up. After all, we had been charged quite a bit extra for this touch of luxury.

We did have to contact the owners, however, as the water was cloudy and scummy with bubbles, and the water needed a jolly good clean. We had a small pool and a Jacuzzi at home, so Ian knew about water management. It turned out that we didn't use it much, what with everything else that happened in this week, and Ian's parents didn't use it at all.

When we had to clean up at the end of our stay, we knew there was a well-stocked cupboard of cleaning materials in the utility room. It was only when we had done our bit of it that David, who is a fanatical cleaner, admitted that, when last they were at the local shops, he had purchased bleach, and had used it with abandon. What a pity we had not explained to him about the *fosse septique* (septic tank). We just sort of assumed that he would know. He had probably murdered it, and it was with a feeling of guilt that we left for the airport.

Even our journey back had the man's inimical stamp on it. We had decided to eat in Bergerac on the way back to the airport, and used the little restaurant we had popped into on the journey to the villa. Having perused the menu, David cornered a waiter who spoke some English, and pointed out the meal we had just ordered, as the same meal was being delivered to another table.

It was a steak with salad and mashed potatoes with small pieces of orange and capers. Very slowly and deliberately, he explained that he wanted his steak well done, that he didn't want the salad, and that he preferred chips to mashed potatoes with some fancy rubbish mixed in. He'd managed to eliminate all the French touches and get English steak and chips.

On our way afterwards, we had to stop to ask directions and, of course, he said he'd do it, unfortunately stopping a very elderly Frenchman. When addressed in Geordie English, the old man just turned and walked away without a word. I think David felt the same. He had not enjoyed the holiday at all.

SURPRISE DECISION, SURPRISE CHATEAU, AND SURPRISE TEABAGS

We returned home without ever talking about the wreck with the *columbage*, but, a few nights later, I said, after lights-out in bed, 'And I suppose we're just too cowardly to take on a property that needs so much doing to it, without a regular income?'

After a brief and ratty discussion, we came to the conclusion that we were. The subject resurfaced a couple of days later, as we were both bursting with the thought of the place, and we came to a rather shaky decision, especially as this was 2007, just before the financial crisis. Ian declared that, on checking, the tiny village seemed to have Internet access. He would be able to trade on the stock market as he had done in the past, and if he took voluntary redundancy, we should be able to get by.

We phoned the agent again and said we'd like to have a second viewing, only to be told that another English couple were coming back as well, as they were thinking of re-opening the restaurant. Help! When were they coming?

We'd be there first. We promptly booked flights for a few days before the other couple were due to come back. There are no rules. All's fair in love and war, and we were in love.

The next problem was, where would we stay? We'd had the rented villa to stay in before, so Ian got on the Internet again, and eventually came out of the study to inform me that he'd found a *chambre d'hôte* called the *Château de Puy Ferat*. We thought, as there was no accompanying picture, that this would turn out to be a pretentious semi with delusions of grandeur, but at least it would be a bed for the nights we would be staying there, and it wasn't too far from our prospective new house.

On our drive down there, we made jokes about loo roll holders with coats of arms, and suits of armour to hang our clothes on. We really let rip at the thought of an ordinary house calling itself a chateau. Imagine our faces, then, when we saw signs for the place we sought, eventually turning off the road on to a drive that must have been half a mile long.

The chateau was sixteenth-century, and we were its only guests for the night, as well as a brace of scornful disbelieving nincompoops. The owners, in their halting English, informed us that the evening meal (with wine, 25 euros) would not be available tonight, as they were going to a party. They did have a social life, didn't we know? And left us to it, the only two human presences in a huge stone-built castle.

I would normally have been quite spooked by the thought, but buying a house and moving to France permanently was a much more frightening proposition, so I just took it in my stride, much to Ian's relief; coping with an event that would otherwise have seen me climbing the walls with fear.

I woke up the following morning, facing away from the bed, and felt Ian sit down (quite heavily) on his side of it, presumably after his shower. Then I heard him singing *in the shower*!!! Keeping my cool to a remarkable degree, I thought maybe it had been the owners' cat, only to remember that it would have to have been able to open two heavy doors with turn handles to get to our room.

At breakfast I spoke to the couple who owned and ran it, asking them if the chateau had a ghost. '*Of course* it has a ghost!' replied Monsieur Château, putting his nose in the air and wandering off as if he had much more important business to attend to than answering stupid questions posed by an English guest.

We went off to the house again and felt even more enthusiastic at this meeting. The agent, speaking no English, had brought her English neighbour with her to translate. The price was too high, although we didn't know it had already been reduced considerably and, eventually we got the owner down to twenty-five thousand euros below the current asking price. This was just as well, as the buyer pays the estate agent in France. As we were selling a house in the UK, we would have two sets of estate agent's fees to pay. In France it is around nine per cent of the purchase price, and we still had to find the *notaire's* (solicitor's) fees.

The estate agent had brought the ingredients of a delicious picnic, including wine and local strawberries as well as fabulous pastries, of which we partook on the mouldering decking, feeling like royalty that has just purchased its first palace.

I could already foresee what both the exterior and interior would look like and actually burst into tears when the owner had agreed to our final offer, announcing, 'We have just bought the house I'm going to die in.' I should coco. This may be a new adventure, but I sincerely hope it won't be my last.

We raised wine glasses to each other, happy in the knowledge that it was us who had arrived first, and secured a firm price on the property. All we had to do was be whisked off by the estate agent and the owner, that very evening, to see the French equivalent of a solicitor, to get the initial details sorted out, and let her know that we needed a pre-sale marital agreement, so that when one of us died, half of the property would not be inherited by and split between our children. It was imperative to do this, and have it legally agreed that the surviving spouse inherited it, so that the children couldn't oust him or her and sell the house from under their feet. Families do fall out, you know.

We went back to look at the house one final time and found ourselves sitting in the car by the gates, dazed at the audacity of what we had done, and watching another hare lope lazily down the traffic-free road through the village.

We had assumed that, as we were so out of the way, the other residents of our little *bourg* would be French. We had heard the lady across the way shouting at her dog, and that was definitely not in English. We had not yet had the pleasure of meeting the residents of the house behind the church, but heard the man calling to the post lady and decided to eavesdrop.

He definitely called to her in French, but seemed to have an unconventional accent. As the post lady began her side of the conversation, we discovered why he spoke like this. He was English, and his French was rudimentary in the extreme. Deciding to follow this up, we waited for the post lady to drive off, then hurried across the road and down the cul-de-sac calling, 'Monsieur! Monsieur!' just in case our ears had deceived us.

They hadn't, and he was indeed from the north of England and he and his wife had been living in their house for about two years. Paul proved to be a very hospitable neighbour, and immediately asked us in to meet his wife Denise and take some refreshment.

Their house was in an immaculate state, and made us

feel just a twinge of jealousy when he explained all the work they had put in to get it that way, as we chatted over our cups of tea, made with English teabags, I hasten to add. The obtaining of these luxurious little squares would take up a lot of time and ingenuity for some time to come, the French equivalent being like sawdust, with neither colour nor flavour.

But, back to the cups of tea. As we enjoyed a proper cuppa, the French lady from next door called round, and there was a rapid conversation in French which made my ears disbelieve what they were hearing. Not only did our new female English neighbour speak French fluently, but she spoke it with a Nottingham accent, giving it a bizarre skew that we could never have imagined had we not heard it for ourselves.

It had been a hot day, there was virtually no traffic, and later, when we viewed the video Ian had taken, the only sound was loud birdsong.

WHAT PRICE LOYALTY, WE DECIDE TO FLEE

We had one more visit to make before the exchange of contracts, when we would set the completion date, and we soon found ourselves flying back again to stay in the chateau. It was very cheap and, although far from luxurious, it had a certain class about it that appealed to my sense of snobbery. This time they did provide dinner – their social calendar must have been a bit empty – and the food was absolutely gorgeous.

The dining room was straight out of medieval times with huge oak dressers, stone-flagged floors and gigantic wrought-iron chandeliers. We were the only diners, as again we were the only guests in the chateau. They started by giving us some sort of concoction in an unmarked bottle as an aperitif which was simply delicious and very potent! Up until that time I had never had the 'pleasure' of eating *gésiers* (gizzards), but that was the starter (they didn't offer a menu, you got what they were serving) and the female half of the couple who owned it had a way of frying them until they were crispy, then serving them over poached eggs with a Madeira sauce that was to die for. Next came a version of Yorkshire pudding, with foie gras in it, served with *dauphinoise* potatoes and French beans which was divine. We finished up with a melange of fruit and meringue with outrageously heavy cream. All this served with local wine, again in unmarked bottles, which was delicious. To send us on our way happily to bed they served a wicked *eau de vie* over a lump of sugar suspended over the coffee cups on the open-work bowls of antique silver absinthe spoons. We slept well that night!

The following day the legal work at the *notaire's* passed without incident, although the enormity of the decision we were now legally committed to must have affected me more than I thought, because I nearly fainted when we came out of her office, and I had to be helped back to the car.

The last hurdle we had to get over was when Ian's company informed us that they would not be paying him his redundancy package, which we discovered, to our delight, would be accompanied by a small pension, until the twelfth of September. This was a huge problem to us, as we had declared that we would complete on the first, which would be our thirty-fourth wedding anniversary, and we thought it would be romantic. Where's Cupid when you need him?

Ian set up an appointment with the bank to talk to them about a bridging loan for the missing twelve days. He assumed that this would not be a problem as he had all the documentation from his company that guaranteed his pay-out. He talked to the local bank manager and all seemed straightforward. Imagine our astonishment when head office turned down our request. We had been loyal customers of the same bank for over thirty years and Ian was almost incandescent with rage that they didn't seem able to return the loyalty. This was at the beginning of the financial crisis and signalled what was about to happen to many small businesses and individuals in the coming months. It left us with a problem.

We needn't have worried. The owner had no objection whatsoever moving the completion date eleven days; so we now knew this new adventure was a real one and not just a pipe dream, the way it turned out to be for so many other couples.

We completed the purchase in September, and looked forward to moving in before Christmas. On such whims as digging in my heels to look at the ugly property, in an area where we couldn't afford to live, in a country I would rather have stuck pins in my eyes than live in, we had found our future.

Our English house, although immaculate and wanted by the first buyer who saw it, was now back on the market, as our buyer had lost his buyer and, instead of moving before Christmas, we were in limbo while the property market collapsed round our ears.

We had various viewings, but the first couple lived in hope that we would not sell it to someone else before they had a new purchaser for their house. Alas, they were not to complete the sale and, at lunch at a race course with Ian's parents, his father's suggestion was the wisest I think he has ever made. 'Why don't you just go now?' he asked.

'What? Just leave the property empty?'

'Why not? Is it cheaper to live here or there?'

We thought about it. The French property was about twice the floor area (with barn extra) than ours, and we had bought a lot of new furniture for it which was currently in storage and costing us.

That weekend, we worked out what our bills were, and what they would be and, hey presto, it was cheaper to live in France. We only needed to take over personal things and our new furniture, so we could leave the house looking furnished and, if we could persuade someone to keep a regular check on the place, it would stay looking as if the owner was simply not around for a few hours. I managed to persuade a good friend who also planned to move to France within the next couple of years to pop in once a week, and keep the lawn looking tidy.

We decided that this would be our last Christmas in England, arranged for all our children and some of our closest friends to come and stay for some time over the holidays, and booked a removal firm and a ferry for the thirteenth of January. Our new lives were about to start.

CHAPTER TWO

OMG!; Meeting the neighbours; First wood delivery; Bringing home the cats; No hot water and no power supply for the cooker; First visitors

OMG!

We took the overnight ferry that would disembark us in France on the fourteenth of the month. We had a long drive ahead of us, but Ian had assured us of overnight accommodation when we arrived.

He had had the brass neck to call the mobile phone number of the couple we had met who lived behind the church, incidentally disturbing the woman at the hairdresser's, and asking her if we could stay with them for our first night as the furniture wouldn't arrive until the next day.

She had only ever spoken to us when they had furnished us with a very welcome cup of tea; the shock of his cheek must have made her agree, so we headed straight for their house when we arrived.

We did take the keys and have a quick look round our new home, and I felt my courage shrivelling and dying when I saw just exactly what we had paid what I thought was an enormous amount of money for. It was a veritable wreck of a building.

Back at the neighbours' house, they fed us with authentic French onion soup, but so uptight was I with fear, that I don't remember the main course or the dessert. I do, however, remember a great deal of red wine poured down four enthusiastic necks, and the next day I, at least, felt like hell.

A walk across the road took us to our new abode, and we found the delivery lorry parked outside, it having arrived towards ten o'clock the previous evening. I went straight into the dining room while Ian opened the double front doors, so that Kynaston's merry crew (the removal men) could start bringing in the furniture we had brought with us. At that time, the only way the front doors could be secured was with a padlock on the outside. What we should do that evening, I had no idea.

I stood in the dining room, looking around me at the bare stone walls with their crumbling lime mortar and clay pointing, at the tired floor tiles with an area still of the underlying wooden floor, where the bar used to be, its staircase with no banister rail, and the antediluvian woodburner that lurked menacingly in the fireplace: the most ugly piece of metal and glass that I had ever seen.

Here and there on the walls were areas of plaster that had resisted the previous owner's enthusiasm for ripping the house to shreds and, on these, were old patches of hand-stamped decoration, rather like that done by a child in the reception class, with poster paint and half a potato.

Climbing four very worn wooden steps to the middle room, I surveyed the plastic kitchen sink and the plastic shower cubicle, both coyly shielded from public gaze by small runs of salmon-pink planks, forming a make-shift modesty screen for each. The floor was fibre-board, as we already knew, but it was only at that point that I remembered the original details had specified wood flooring throughout.

By my reckoning, that was only inaccurate by about 100%. Stop! The two inter-connecting bedrooms did, indeed, have wooden floors, albeit at a crazy angle that made me feel drunk every time I visited them. Make that about 83%. The dining room had an incomplete covering of horrible old tiles, the middle room had a fibreboard floor, and the third room downstairs had a wooden floor that was so rotten that it actually swayed when walked on, which produced a feeling of nausea akin to travel sickness.

The largest upstairs area also had what had once been floorboards, but were now a death-trap of rot and worm, and were unfit for the purpose for which they were originally intended. This was a rich vein of dishonesty to which even English estate agents would not stoop. We had been guilty of not paying enough attention, having got swept up in the moment. This part of the house, which represented about two-thirds of the total upstairs space, had no electricity either, let alone walls, ceilings or doors.

Oh, my God! What had we done? I thought, as I remembered the freshly decorated, immaculate house we had vacated only two nights before. Every room was pristine, with carpet throughout, every room with a ceiling fan, and all the white goods built-in, in either the kitchen or the utility room.

The double garage had held our Jacuzzi and gym equipment, with a tall fridge next to the Jacuzzi holding a supply of white wine. There had also been an elegant conservatory big enough for a seating and a dining area, and a real boon when we had had a barbecue on the patio, or had just got out of the pool.

Here, we had two-thirds of an acre of wilderness, no foundations, hardly any electricity or plumbing, no central heating, and only one working wood-burner between us and the ravages of the French winter. Was I out of my mind? Whatever had possessed me to agree to live in this – this hovel – this wreck – this dilapidated ruin? How had I ended up in this, the last country on earth in which I would have chosen to live?

But panic had to be temporarily shelved, as Kynaston's lads were racing in and out of the front door carrying armfuls of our possessions, and the next few hours were a time for instructions, not whinging. 'Not up there! Put it in the room next to the barn.' 'Don't bring that into the house. To the barn, now!' 'Mind the corners! That's brand new, I'll have you know.'

In fact, much of the stuff we had brought over in this first adventure with Kynaston and his lads was brand new. The new (ha ha!) house was three hundred square metres, the barn two hundred, not counting its upstairs, and we needed a lot of stuff to make it look like it was even part-furnished.

The new furniture, as I mentioned before, had been purchased specially for this new life and had lived for some months in two large storage units and, from the old (new!) house, we had only brought our personal possessions, and things like the computer that would not be missed, along with anything that would help make any of the rooms we were leaving behind look less cluttered.

We had, actually, left it looking like someone had just popped out for a newspaper, and would be back at any minute. There's nothing so depressing as an empty house, when it's for sale and empty with all the furniture dents in the carpet leering at prospective buyers.

The friend who had offered to pop in and check there were no problems had also kindly offered to mow the lawns when necessary, and we had left her a petrol mower with which to achieve this end, with the minimum of inconvenience to herself, telling her that she could keep the mower as a thank you when we sold. Fortunately we had no flower beds to fret about, as the garden maintenance had been kept to an absolute minimum, given the amount of time we were away on holiday, playing Lord and Lady Muck.

Now we had two thousand five hundred square metres (count them! one, two, three ...) of armpit-high dried-out weeds from goodness knows how many springs and summers of total neglect. I was convinced the garden at the back of the barn was really small, until Ian started to clear it, and then it just went on and on and on, revealing a mini streamlet that wound its way across, and trees that we had no idea existed.

If you ever need to move, may I suggest that you Google Mr Kynaston from Welshpool, because not only does he give you a very fair price, he also goes above and beyond the call of duty in his services. That first full day, he worked like a slave. If something had gone up the wrong set of stairs, and there was no connection between the two upstairs areas, he didn't even sigh. He just got on with taking it back down the stairs he had taken it up, then right through the house, and up the other flight of stairs.

He and his boys were nothing short of a miracle and not only did we use him for the second part of our move, and for an unexpected order for two extra sideboards, but he has also been used by two friends of ours, then individuals, and will shortly be used again by them, now, as a couple. I have used his real name, because I think he deserves the public plaudits.

Back in the immediate world, though, I found myself going up the north staircase clutching two boxes containing the light fittings for the two inter-connecting bedrooms, one of which would be ours, until we had converted the other side from a barn into a space fit for human habitation.

Imagine my consternation when I put down my boxes, looking forward to seeing their contents fitted, and looked up to find that there were no ceiling light fittings in this end of the upstairs either. I just hadn't noticed before, so great was my trepidation at leaving England to live in the land of one of our oldest historic enemies.

We fed the team of three removals men that night, as our new abode was in the middle of nowhere, the nearest town fifteen kilometres away. They would sleep in the van, as they had done the night before, and leave after breakfast. We would sleep in our new six-feet-wide hand-made fruit-wood sleigh bed, the carrying of which up a narrow staircase with a turn in it, had produced more bad language than I had heard since we had had a twenty-stone leather double sofa bed delivered to our previous home, and told the delivery men that we wanted it taken up to the first floor, via a staircase that had a one hundred and eighty degree turn.

The bed was only one part of a range from which we had selected numerous items. Although expensive, they were top quality, and we thought we really ought to buy furniture that would outlive us, as we'd probably never have any money for the rest of our lives. We had chosen to live on about six per cent of what our joint income was before Ian chose to accept voluntary redundancy, and the only money we would have coming in now would be the tiny pension that he didn't even know he was going to get, not having considered the fact that he was over fifty.

When we had found out, however, we had done a little dance together round our old kitchen, singing, 'I've been made redundant! I've been made redundant!' What a jolly jape it had seemed at the time, but now it was real. When we had bought the property the previous September, the exchange rate was €1.40 to the pound. In four months, it had dropped to €1.20, and that would make a serious difference to the pittance we were proposing to live on, but that was not of the highest priority, on our arrival.

Things would get better, wouldn't they? And we had a buyer for our house, although his buyer had withdrawn from the chain. Surely it would only be a case of waiting for him to secure a new purchaser, then we could get on with things, and get in the builders. How naïve we were, and how much worse things were going to get, before they got better. I thank God that there was no way we could have seen into the future, because, had that been possible, I think we would have packed that van again, and asked Mr Kynaston to drive like hell for the UK and not stop until he was across the Channel once more, outside our lovely modern house.

The house devoured our furniture, and still looked hungry when the last few things had been manhandled in, the next morning.

Eventually Kynaston's crew lined up ready to make their farewells, John somehow had managed to locate the Russian Army officer's hat we had purchased in St Petersburg a few years ago, and he stood to attention between his two lads, saluting us, as I rushed for the camera. We made our *au revoirs* knowing that we would see them again with the rest of our furniture when our house in the UK was sold (and there would be absolutely no possibility of going back!).

As the enormous truck poked its front out of our gateway, John K beckoned for Ian to come to the cab window. 'The satnav won't work,' he explained, 'unless I'm actually on a road, so I don't know which way to turn.'

'No problem,' said Ian. 'Just tell me where you want to go, and I'll point you in the right direction.' There was absolutely no clue that Kynaston was setting him up for a last little jape.

'Geneva,' he replied, then roared with laughter.

Without flinching or changing his facial expression, Ian replied coolly, 'Turn right, and keep on until you hit the *route nationale*, and by then your satnav should be functioning perfectly. Have a good trip!'

Ian's house-point, I rather think!

THE FIRST FULL DAY

Paul very kindly offered to come over to our wreck and show Ian how to get the fire going, but the dratted thing would hardly draw, and his wife, Denise, very kindly got in touch with her French chimney sweep who agreed to call round as soon as he could, to see what was causing the problem. I suppose, in January, there is not much call for this service, as the majority of people have their chimneys swept in the summer, when there is no need to run the fire. Consequently, he arrived within the hour, collecting Denise on his way, to interpret.

There were three chimneys in the house in all, and we left him to it as he set to, to clear whatever obstruction was hindering our efforts to keep warm. While we lugged pieces of furniture into position and opened boxes mysteriously labelled 'tractor' and 'tractor trailer' by Kynaston, the sweep solved the mystery of the lack of drawing-power of the only working wood-burner in the house.

It had (and still has) a pipe at the back leading into the chimney, with the diameter of a dinner plate; adequate space, one would have thought, to draw air to nurture the flames, and we had been under the impression that it was a requirement of French insurance companies that chimneys were to be swept every summer, or any claims regarding the chimney would not be met.

'Zis chim-en-ay 'as not bin swept since ze war,' he informed us, in much better English than we could have managed in French. 'Ze 'ole in zat beeg fat pipe was only about ze size of a twenty centime coin.' (Twenty pence piece is the nearest equivalent.)

He had, in fact, removed so much soot that he was unable to take it all away, and a good deal of it had to be transferred to a shameful pile, out of sight, behind the barn. The other two chimneys were in a somewhat better state, but that was probably because it was impossible to use the fires that sat in their grates.

One of them, the monster I mentioned earlier, looked too scary to light. I expected it to blow up if we attempted anything stupid like lighting it. The one in the room we eventually referred to as the *séjour* was a tall, old-fashioned, wide cylinder, with decorative ironwork around its glass insert and on its lid.

It was set about six feet into the room, its pipe making a barrier to crossing the room in front of the mantelpiece, but Ian soon solved that. Thank God we didn't try to get it going though, because, on inspection, the small panels of glass, that were one's view on how the fire was burning, turned out to be a cunning substitution with cellophane. We'd probably have burnt the place to the ground.

We'd had to beg to get the previous owner to leave the large burner in the middle room, but she was quite happy to leave the other two. No wonder! She also 'did us over' with an agreed insurance claim, but that's a totally different story (see later). When we were about to move in, we had been informed that there were some cut logs in the barn, and did we want to purchase them for thirty euros? Ian, of course, said no – she'd never bother to take *those* with her.

She did, apart from a few scraps, and we now urgently needed a delivery of wood. She even took the huge chunks of stone that had been knocked out of the back wall of the second section of the barn to add on what was now an extremely squalid and out-dated shower room.

FIRST WOOD DELIVERY

Our kind and generous neighbour also offered to get in touch with his wood supplier, and have a load delivered that would see us through the winter. More problems! How much did we want? How the hell did we know, having previously only received warmth and comfort during our many years of marriage from electricity, gas, and oil? Wood was a completely unknown area for us, and then we discovered that it could be ordered by the 'brass' or the 'steer'. I could have wept, and, once more, we relied on Paul's experience to guide us.

An old open-backed truck drove on to our property the next day, and lifted its back section, to deposit something like eight cubic metres of oak logs, all a metre long, and in one hell of a messy pile, right outside the barn. Ian took one look at it and declared that it had to be stacked in the area he had designated to be his 'wood barn', and the neighbours very kindly gave us a hand.

It rained! Oh, how it rained! 'We need to get the wood out of the rain, otherwise it won't burn!' yelled Ian, stating the bleedin' obvious. It took a couple of hours for four people and several wheelbarrows to move it. I would have thought it might have taken longer, but we hadn't realised yet that, as it hadn't been wired up in cubic metres, we'd been 'done' on the quantity, and a lot of it was light. Too light! It was rotten, and should not have been sold to us at that price. It was our first case of 'fleece the newbies', but only a minor one compared to what happened next.

BRINGING HOME THE CATS

Moving ourselves and all our worldly possessions to another country wasn't all we had to do. We also had cats. We've always had cats. In fact, we've had cats longer than we've had children. Living the high life, as we had been, three of these were no ordinary cats. The only moggie, Merlin, had been a whim on my part, as I shall explain. When the last of our old cats finally died, we decided that we would have no more. Such a stern undertaking was this, that we lasted all of twenty-four hours before beginning to plan our new pride.

Rumours of the possibilities of taking voluntary redundancy had started a full twelve months before we had moved, and, as Ian at least already had a firm resolve to move across the Channel, we had, when the last of our moggies had left us at the grand old age of nearly nineteen, indulged ourselves with the purchase of two brown-spotted

Bengal boys, which we named Ludo(vic) and Dom(inic). He also warmed the cockles of his heart with dreams of this pair of wild things haring through the French countryside, having the time of their lives wreaking havoc and death wherever they went.

Ludo – only six months old – had been hit by a car when we were out here on holiday, and was dead. When we returned home we had him cremated, and kept his ashes, to be scattered where his brother would eventually live.

Six months later, just shy of his first birthday, a farmer from the next village called us to say he thought he had found our cat – at least, he thought it was a cat, and would Ian come over and identify him. Poor Dominic had been killed on the road, and been run over by goodness knows how many other vehicles, before the farmer kindly lifted what was left of him on a shovel, and gave him a decent burial on the farm.

We had also bought a silver-spotted Bengal whose pedigree name we had been allowed to choose, and I had named her Perfect Cadence, because she struck a chord in my soul, and whenever I held her on visits to the breeder, I shook like a leaf, with love.

The deaths of both spotty boys left us with one cat, and we could never be happy with an only cat, because it didn't seem fair that the animal had no other feline company or playmate, so we duly acquired Merlin. He was an accident.

Cadence had been taken to the vet to have her second lot of jabs, when I saw a trio of kittens in a wicker basket, also waiting to see the vet, and just had a tiny peek inside. And there he was: an adorable tiny grey and white kitten with a face that made me giggle, as it reminded me of Nicholas Lyndhurst. I was smitten, and, while Ian was in the consultation room with Cadence, I made a swift deal with the woman whose kitten it was, who was just getting them checked over for re-homing, and took my place in the consultation room with an unexpected little bundle in my arms.

With a casual, 'Could you just do this fellow, too?' I put him down on the table, and Ian's mouth dropped wide open.

'What on earth have you done?' he asked, unable to believe his eyes.

'I've just adopted this kitten, and he's ours now.'

At this point, the woman who, until a few minutes ago had been his owner, popped her head round the door and informed us that he liked a little evaporated milk with warm water, and that she and her children had called him 'Snowy'.

Surveying him with a critical eye, I metaphorically spat on the name 'Snowy', and promptly renamed him Merlin. He seemed to be a wizard little kitten, and needed a name to reflect this.

The next cat to join our family was an Abyssinian who rejoiced, after a few days with us, in the name of Monkey. She took to me in particular, and she would sit on my shoulder as I walked around, and put her arms around my neck when sitting on my chest, to 'kiss' me with her cheeks.

Making up a quartet was child's play, as Cadence's breeder had had a sale fall through, and so her brother Marbles (a marbled Bengal) joined us shortly afterwards. He became particularly attached to Ian, and followed him everywhere he went. They always sat together in the evenings, Marbles making quite a bulk on his knees, for he was turning into a very large cat. His father was absolutely enormous when we met him at the breeder's, and I hoped he wouldn't be quite that big when he grew up.

Starting the day before our possessions were packed, they had embarked on an adventure of their own, being collected by a specialist courier, shipped to France, and installed in a cattery not too far from our new home. They were only to be there for a week, but we extended this to ten days when we realised exactly how much work we would have to do before we were in a fit state to welcome them to their new home, and give our time to them to settle them in.

Before we moved, the little devils would only eat wet food, turning their noses up in disdain at anything else, and would make the very devil of a mess of my lovely shiny kitchen floor while eating. When we collected them from their temporary home at the cattery, they had happily eaten dry food for ten days, with no fuss whatsoever. We didn't know whether to laugh or cry, but this was a welcome change in their diet, as wet food would not fare well in the heat of a French summer, and the flies it would attract would be unhealthy, as well as unbearable.

We had planned to keep them in for seven to ten days, so that they became familiar with their new surroundings, but they, of course, had other ideas, and Ian found himself fitting a cat flap within two days of their installation. They wanted to go out, and would achieve this end by hook or by crook, so we gave in, and let them have their freedom, hoping that they would remember where they lived when they got hungry. Of course they did!

So, now the whole tribal group was assembled, and we were champing at the bit to learn what we could about life abroad.

NO HOT WATER AND NO POWER SUPPLY FOR THE COOKER

The title of this section shows two other problems it was vital to solve in January, in a large stone house that had not been lived in for a year, and had only one wood-burner with which to warm its stones.

On a previous visit, we had met with an architect

(whom it turned out we didn't need, but he forbore to mention that to us before we had paid him 6,000 euros – the exact amount for which I had given away my lovely Mercedes SLK (leather interior, personalised number plates, multi-CD player, low mileage!), prior to moving here, but that, again, is another story.

With him had come a representative of the building company with which he worked in tandem. The representative of the builders, whom I shall use the initial letters to refer to as ROB, we had taken an instant dislike to. He'd sneered at our house, beginning with the dining room with the exposed stone.

I agreed with him that it was not very pretty (it will actually be worked on next month. It's taken a bit of time to get round to), but he insisted that it would need to be sand-blasted to within an inch of its life. Already I didn't like him.

In the middle room, he had looked around with a sneer and said there was a helluva lot of work to do, but on entering the *séjour*, (drawing room) he committed the sin that was one of the two occurrences that lost his company the job for the refurbishment. (Some things we just could not tackle ourselves, and intended to pay for, not only for speed and convenience, but so that they didn't look as if we *had* done them ourselves!)

He looked at my wonderful, ancient *columbage* wall – and rubbished it, commenting instantly that it was obviously a fake, as they don't have that sort of thing around here – only further north! They damned well do, you know, buddy. It's a feature of the forested area.

This wall leaned at an angle that couldn't have been faked. The timbers were bent with hundreds of years of keeping the house upright. How could he say they were fakes? This man didn't know what he was talking about, and, apart from taking an instant dislike to him, our unease grew.

The hot water tank simply didn't work, however, and there was no way we could run the cooker without a very stout piece of wiring being installed, something that Ian didn't want to tackle, being rather wary of what wiring did exist, and its ultimate safety. The only man we knew was this shady character, so, we thought, how much can it cost, even if the immersion tank has to be replaced, to do that and fit a hefty wire for our cooker? In January we were in desperate need of both hot water and hot food.

So we called ROB, and he duly sent round Weedy and Whistler, both, of course, without a word of English. Don't believe anybody who says that everyone in France speaks English!. It is an out-and-out lie and, even if they do, some people will pretend that they don't, just to see you squirm.

Weedy, in mime, declared the immersion tank dead ('Mort! Mort!'), and sent Whistler off to get another one, which I later suspected was concealed in their van. At the time I believed he had gone on a thirty kilometre round-trip to buy a new one, but later I suspected that he had merely driven the van out of sight, smoked a few Gauloises, and then driven back round the corner. No receipt was ever produced.

Whistler, meanwhile, fitted an enormously thick black (!) wire to our electricity supply in the dining room, and then had to drill a hole through the adjoining wall to the area we had designated the kitchen. The wall was twenty-eight and a half inches thick! I measured it! Boy was that a long drill, but instead of making the hole in the wall down near the floor, where it would be less noticeable, he drilled it about a foot from the ceiling. The cooker was twenty-three feet away, at the other end of the room, and he whistled while he drilled a series of holes (in the side wall?) all the way down the room, then turned left and headed for the cooker.

Now happy with his handiwork, he put stout nails in the holes, and draped the thick black connecting wire along it, and connected it to the cooker. What a delightful addition to the already atrocious décor that was. Meanwhile, Weedy had arrived back from his pretend shopping trip, and fitted the new water tank under the stairs next to the ghastly little loo cubicle. All done, and in less than an hour and a half. Not tidily done. Not aesthetically pleasing, but done, nevertheless. Little did we know, at the time, that the water tank needed only a new element.

Babes in the wood, we thanked them and were glad to see the back of them, with absolutely no idea of what we had just done. A week later the bill arrived.

For ONE THOUSAND SEVEN HUNDRED EUROS!!!

Most people may be kind and helpful, but you need to remember that to some, you are nothing more than a sitting duck! In French, that's a *bonne poire* – or a good pear! I thought we were more of a right pair, to let this happen to us, but we were learning.

FIRST VISITORS

Ten days after we arrived, we collected two very good English friends, Kay and Robert, from the local airport. They, too, were bent on a life in la belle France, and couldn't wait to get over and see what we had bought, even offering to spend most of their time helping us to unpack, move furniture around, and anything else that needed doing, provided that they could view a few properties, as they wanted to move as near to us as possible. How sweet!

They were completely without unrealistic expectations, and had even viewed the photographs of the house we had taken before moving in, so were consequently not shocked at the ragged and neglected state of our new home. Their funds were limited, and they thought it would be good practice for when they found somewhere for themselves.

That would not be for a while, however, as there was the small matter of two divorces to sort out, before the actual state of their joint finances was revealed.

Kay and Robert were enchanted by the house and its potential. (It may not have had much, at the moment, but, boy did it have potential – in spades!) They weren't even fazed when we showed them to their sleeping quarters and explained that that part of the house had no water supply, so if they were in need of a lavatory at night, all they had to do was go down the staircase with no handrail (in the dark), then through the dining room, up the steps to the middle room, being careful not to let through any of our four cats, then into the entrance hall, turn right – *et voila*!

In order to provide them with a choice, however, there were a couple of china commodes in the room, which they were welcome to use, should they not wish to risk life and limb, staggering about in the dark, in a strange house, in the middle of the night.

The two of them worked like slaves while they were with us, wading into the wilderness that was the garden with Ian, while I stayed inside unpacking boxes. I remember one particular day, when they were determined that Ian should have his first vegetable bed, not just recovered from the wilderness, but dug and planted before they left, and I was in the dining room unpacking glassware to fill one of our many sideboards.

We knew, from the two days we had spent with them, that there was a mischievous side to our removal men, and a discovery in one of the boxes of glassware showed that they had left us a little joke to remember them by when they were gone. Most of the glassware had come from a glass-fronted tall cupboard that sat to the left of the kitchen sink in the old house, with the toaster in between. If we had muffins or crumpets left over from a Saturday breakfast, they would be rolled up in their packaging, and slipped into this cupboard for the next day.

I couldn't remember exactly when we had last had the buttery treat of muffins, but after a run of glassware of various sizes, I pulled a very light bundle of packing paper from the box, and unwrapped it to find A MUFFIN. Beginning to laugh, I determined not to be distracted, and removed the next bundle of paper and, lo and behold, it was *another* muffin. The two were as hard as concrete, but I could easily have softened them with the tears of mirth that streaked down my cheeks as I held one in each hand and stared at them in disbelief.

Unbelievably, three little beds were cleared and dug during that week (my friend Kay said it was the only way to keep warm, staying outdoors and working like a dog), the front and side lawns were hacked down and mown, and the first fruit tree planted, all thanks to the kind and industrious assistance of these two hard-working friends of ours.

We kept our part of the bargain, however, and took them into the nearest town and into the largest of the estate agents' offices. In there, we were lucky enough to meet an English woman who had lived for over thirty years in the country, and was not only able to help us choose properties to view, but to come with us on most of the visits and do all the translation necessary.

Towards the end of our conversation with her, she asked a little about us, as we had just moved to the area, and asked if she could pass my name and telephone number on to another couple who had moved to the area about fourteen months before. They were involved with a lot of music round and about, and she thought it would help us if we got to know them. I was game for that. Anything musical would be right up my alley, and it was a good way of meeting people with the same interests. But more of this later.

Nothing came of those initial viewings, as they all proved totally unsuitable, and we rather thought she had rounded up all the properties on the agency's books that had become stuck there for some time, and tried her luck with us. Never mind, though, as we all had a jolly good laugh.

One property we visited just outside the town sticks in my mind because we passed it every time we went into town, and it had been for sale since the first time we had visited the area.

It had a vast amount of outbuildings, but windows about the size of a cream cracker. A demoralised woman was in residence with a young child and what we presumed to be her mother, all of them sitting on wooden chairs in a room divided into two small cells with plywood. It was like a scene from Dickens. Her home had been on the market for three years.

The agent explained that the woman was getting divorced, and her husband had started a lot of DIY projects before leaving. Boy, had he done that! Walls were very roughly demolished leaving unsightly holes joining unlikely spaces, and he had even removed part of the staircase, so that the only way to view the rooms on the first floor was by a collection of haphazardly placed rickety planks. I stayed downstairs. No way was I going to risk life and limb to see the first floor of a house that was obviously a non-starter from the moment we had stepped over the threshold. It had been a wasted and pointless day, but there would be another when we might be luckier.

What wasn't so funny was the heating situation in our home. Kay tried the plastic kitchen-living room shower once. It could only be used when someone had come down to rake out, lay and light the fire, but then, of course, no one could go into the only room with heating, because of the exposed position of the cubicle, and the necessity of being in a state of nakedness while showering.

After only one session, Kay announced that she wasn't getting into that freezing contraption again, and would go home dirty, rather than repeat the experience. She wasn't to be the only one who felt like that about our living conditions, particularly during the cold part of the year.

We had a smallish but new black leather corner group for seating at that time, and no coffee table in front of it, so anyone sitting on it was really close to the log fire. It didn't matter how close one got, though, as the stones of the house had lost all the heat that it usually retained when it was occupied, and, evening after evening, we sat in a little semi-circle, wearing multi-layered clothing, hats, scarves and gloves, and with blankets over our laps. An ice hotel couldn't have been colder, and we began to doubt that we could survive another winter like this, when the temperature finally plunged to minus ten degrees.

After a shopping expedition to purchase a few items of French clothing, Kay announced that she couldn't understand the sizing system on the labels, as they seemed to be just one to four. She had decided, with the experience of our house to inform her, that these were probably the number of the layer of clothing you were wearing, number one being for warm days, and number four, for freezing days, like the ones we were experiencing during her visit. Highly unlikely, but a very practical idea, for it was almost impossible to walk with five layers of clothes on. I know. I tried it.

When Kay and Robert fled for more clement conditions in their warm English home, they left in such a hurry that a pair of work boots and a thick woolly were found abandoned, after we returned from dropping them off at the airport. They're still here.

They were exhausted and probably suspected imminent frostbite, but they were unbowed, and said they'd come back in the spring, and do some more viewings. What hardy folk, and true friends to boot!

STATUS OF UK HOUSE: Still unsold, but first viewer still wants to buy it, although he has not found a new buyer for his property.

CHAPTER THREE

White goods and white weather; Taming the garden and the trouble with bonfires; Joining a choral society

WHITE GOODS AND WHITE WEATHER

The first ten days of our new life had been filled with torrential rain, falling as if a new flood were on the way, and we had not ordered enough wood to build an ark. I don't think they take orders for cubits here, anyway.

This was followed by a period of intense cold that culminated in a couple of inches of snow, which really surprised us. So far south, we had not expected to have much to do with snow but, nevertheless, there it was, all over the garden, making it look tidy and sparklingly beautiful.

This move to colder weather also dictated what we wore, both during the day and during the night. In the daytime, apart from the essential knickers, the first layer consisted of a thermal vest and thermal long johns (long janes, in my case). Socks were added as a first protection for the feet, and then a thin jumper was put on. On top of this, a heavy jumper was added, and furry slippers for the feet. If we were sitting around, as we did in the evenings, exhausted from our day's labour, a hat, scarf, and gloves or mittens were added to the outfit, and, over the whole, was spread a furry blanket.

Our evenings were sedentary, not only because we were so tired, but because it was so difficult to walk wearing so many layers of clothes! Going to bed was something that I learned, very quickly, to dread. Sleeping in one of the interconnecting bedrooms, as we had to until we had a new suite of rooms built within the walls of the larger portion of the first floor, we had found ourselves on a north-east corner, with only single glazing that had very thin glass, as our sole protection from the temperature.

Taking one's clothes off was torture, and what to wear in bed was quite a decision. I finally settled on taking two hot water bottles, to Ian's one, to bed with me, retaining my thermal vest and knickers, topped with a floor length flannelette nightie and a South American knitted hat with ear-flaps. Mittens were out of the question, because I found that I couldn't turn the pages of my book, and going to sleep without reading was something I found impossible to contemplate.

The very first night we had slept here I was confronted with a commode, because I usually made two or three trips a night to the lavatory, just for a little wee. I fetched the potty from below the chair that partially concealed its presence, I crouched, I started to wee. Ian suddenly shouted 'Why is there water running out from under the bed?' Immediately, I realised that I had missed, and the almost clear liquid had gone with the flow of the floor boards, right over to Ian's side of the room.

I apologised profusely, and managed to crouch with a bit more accuracy, before grabbing a roll of toilet tissue to clear up the mess I had just made. When I got back to my own side of the bed, I was so flustered I knocked a packet of Polo mints on to the floor from my bedside table.

'May I have my mints back, please?' I asked Ian, as the packet had done the same as the wee, and was now on his side of the bed.

You may not believe it, but I repeated the inaccuracy of my aim again the very next night. The day afterwards we went into town to a DIY shop and bought a green two gallon (or whatever that is in continental measurements) bucket.

In the mornings, the same dread as the night before duly arrived at the thought of getting out of nightwear and into daywear. It was time to take off the hat and the nightie, and think about reassembling a suitable number of layers to provide sufficient warmth for the tasks we had planned to do, without hindering our movement to such an extent that we waddled like penguins.

We also needed to do something about the amount of laundry we had accumulated since we had moved here. Everything in our old kitchen had been built in, and although we had purchased a range-cooker before we arrived here, the only other white goods we had were an old freezer, and an even older fridge that used to live in the double garage, to hold the white wine for our Jacuzzi sessions.

We were in urgent need of a washing machine, a tumble dryer and a dishwasher – luxuries I could only be parted from kicking and screaming, and I was determined only to forsake them on my deathbed. That meant a session with the dictionary as, although we had been using what spare time we could afford working on learning French, our vocabulary did not extend to this sort of consumer goods.

I learnt my little spiel like an actress desperate for the part, and we set out for the only white goods shop we had yet come across. The nearest town is really a one-horse place, not even having sufficient choice of shops to be referred to as a *deux chevaux*!

On arrival I made my speech, desperately hoping that my 'will you help me' – *m'aidez* – didn't sound like exactly what it was: Mayday. If I'd had a flare in my pocket, I'd have launched it. I '*je voudrais*-ed' beautifully, and rattled off my list: *lave-linge* (washing machine) *séchoir* (dryer) and *lave-vaisselle* (dishwasher) with as much confidence as I could muster, and found that we were immediately conducted to what we wanted. What a miracle a little knowledge was! We still had to learn the harsh lesson that a little knowledge is also a very dangerous thing.

Ian, being a competent plumber, managed to get them fixed in place, connected up, and working on the day they were delivered, and boy were we glad we had practised reciting the French alphabet just that morning. After selecting the goods, we were asked our name, then how to spell it in French (eff-air-ah-zed-uh-air). We were still announcing ourselves as M et Mme Frazer, not realising that French people would soon, and forever, call us M et Mme FRAH-zair!

Next question, what is your address? Can you spell that for me? Just about! Telephone number? And over to Ian. I can't do numbers in English, let alone another language, so it was his turn to shake the cobwebs off his tongue and do his bit. How sorry I suddenly felt for all the Polish people who had settled in England. I now knew exactly how they felt, isolated in a foreign country, where nothing is understandable, and life is a mystery. We had become Poles!

But, back to the white goods, and Ian had had to install them in the middle room, which was also our kitchen, with a large sitting and TV area, and also with a dining table and six chairs. They certainly knew how to build houses with good-sized rooms in the olden days. This room was fast becoming what we had seen described on French house details as the 'winter sitting room'. As most of the old properties over here don't have central heating (unless bought by someone non-French) everyone retreated to the one room that had a good log-burner during the day for the coldest weather and, without realising it, we had instinctively done the same.

Now, we may have had to turn up the television volume when these things were running in the evening, but it certainly added to the heat in the room, and for this, we were most grateful. We didn't yet have 'plumbed-in' television, because we had to preserve what money we had, as we hadn't sold our UK house, and didn't want to compromise the renovation money we were counting on having. I had, in the 'spirit of the Blitz', spent months recording programmes and transferring them to DVD for our entertainment after we had moved, with the result that we now had over a thousand hours of programmes to choose from, and didn't miss conventional television at all.

I had even – and this is a heroic admission – given up my beloved *Coronation Street*, which I had watched from its first broadcast episode, being allowed to stay up to watch it, as my father was working that evening. I remembered sitting on my mother's knee while we instantly became hooked. Well, no more! I had enough to cope with in this most alien of countries, and I needed no fiction to rival the challenges of reality.

TAMING THE GARDEN AND THE TROUBLE WITH BONFIRES

The back garden was a jungle of weeds from previous years, reaching to chest height. We knew it had been dug up to install a new *fosse septique* (ancient, but very green drainage system) in 2004, but it had recovered from having its soil (clay) churned up, and a veritable jungle arose anew which blew raspberries at us every time we went out of the door at the back of the barn.

The larger of the weeds were really reaching for the sky, and had dried out like sticks. There was only one way to tackle this, and that was the hard way. We didn't have money to spend getting someone else in to do all the back-breaking work; that was down to Ian. This was his dream: he was the one who was auditioning for the part of Adam the gardener. Let him clear his dream plot!

As this was about to start, there was a sudden and

unexpected change in the weather. We began what was to be a month of glorious sunshine and temperatures of 20°C which was completely unknown to us in February! The gloom of the previous month lifted and we began to tell ourselves that this was the sort of thing we had moved to the south of France to experience. We even got sunburnt! Image me sitting on a chair at the back of the barn watching and 'supervising' the clearing of the garden wearing my thermal vest and with my long janes rolled up my legs to get the sun.

And so he started, inch by inch, (or 2.54 cm x 2.54 cm, if you've gone metric) pulling out the matted long grasses and less challenging weeds with a rake, then changing to a tool that would cut through what was left. Then it was the turn of the mattock, to remove large clumps of couch grass, large stones and lumps of concrete. It took him weeks of back-breaking effort to reach the end, and it was only when he was finishing the clearing that I realised I had missed a priceless photographic opportunity. If only I had taken a photograph every few days, I could then have made a story-board picture called, tongue firmly in cheek, 'The Rake's Progress'!

After all this, the digging had to begin, and I think Ian found that this challenge made the clearing of the land look like a walk in the park. Me? I was planting seeds in pots to put in the two cold-frames we had bought. I found that a pleasurable occupation, and saw it as tucking up my babies in bed, so that they could grow while they slept. After all, when he'd finished all that digging, he'd need something to put in the beds, and I was the one who was going to provide him with healthy little plants for his new Eden.

Meanwhile, everything that had been cleared couldn't all go into the four newly built compost bays. Some of it would need to be burnt and, as the weather had now turned more than fair, it was time to have a few bonfires. Ian, of course, was OIC Fires, while I was designated Chief Fire Watcher, a role that I did not take wholly seriously, and pulled up a chair to watch the pretty fire, and generally relax.

I wasn't at all ready, then, when a cry of 'Fire!' went up, and Ian was suddenly yelling at me to grab a spade and beat out the flames. I had not considered that the area where the bonfire was situated was also an area covered in dry grass from the previous year, and now it was on fire, blazing away merrily, and with ambitions to visit other parts of our garden.

By the time I had extinguished it, I smelt like a chimney, and was covered in smuts from the smoke. So much for quietly sitting and contemplating!

JOINING A CHORAL SOCIETY

The lady in the estate agent's had been as good as her word and, about ten days after I had given her my name and contact number, I got a telephone call. The caller identified himself as Andrew Chandler and immediately launched into an enthusiastic monologue about the opportunities hereabouts for people who wanted to take part in musical activities.

He gave me details of a local choral society which he claimed (and rightly so, it transpired) was the best in the area. He also chattered on about an amateur orchestra with which he played. The choir met on a Wednesday evening, the orchestra on a Monday, and would I like to go to Villamblard to a concert tonight?

I knew how far Villamblard was, having seen signposts for it, and courteously declined. We were still exhausted every evening. In fact, it was only the evening before, as we sat on the leather corner group, that I turned to Ian and said, 'But we can't go to bed now. It's only half past six!'

Promising to think about all he'd told me, I hung up,

my head a whirl of rehearsal times and days, and no idea whatsoever what I wanted to dive into, if I wanted to dive into anything at all. Andrew was persistent, however, and made frequent phone calls, all of a persuasive nature, which finally culminated in an invitation for afternoon tea, with directions for how to find their home. I held up my white flag and surrendered. Opposition was obviously useless.

On the appointed day, we found their abode and were admitted to their home, immediately being shown to the kitchen, where afternoon tea was laid out on the table. Andrew and his wife, June, with whom I had also conversed on the phone, sounded a good deal younger than they looked.

We were here almost under false pretences, at fifty-three, as the other retirees we met were considerably older than us. I had had my birthday eight days after we had arrived here. Andrew turned out to be seventy years young, June about eight years younger. On the telephone, conversation had been easy and flowing. Face to face was a very different proposition.

For a while things were rather stilted, and June had the most peculiar body language, holding herself very stiffly, her head slightly to one side, and turning the whole top half of her body, when spoken to. I was unnerved by it, but fought to hide my misgivings. Tea, however, began to thaw things, and the conversation flowed a little more naturally as time ticked by.

By the time we were near the end of the cake and sandwiches, and were discussing bad backs, Andrew did something that, for me, broke the spell of how they looked, and gave me the necessary insight not to judge a book by its cover. To demonstrate something that he used to do to ease pain in his lower back, he suddenly dived down on the floor on his back like a distressed beetle, and began rocking back and forth, giving a running commentary the while about how this provided quick and easy relief.

They were just the same as us, inside their heads! We were always surprised to catch a reflection of ourselves, thinking, who's that old git or old bag? We all four had something in common. As long as our bodies didn't forbid it, we defied our age and acted how we felt, which Andrew Chandler had just proved was a great deal younger than his decreed age. That sealed what was to be a friendship which has lasted to this day, and June's stilted body language was soon after explained by the fact that she suffered severe neck and back pain, and could move no other way.

The more taxing problem for me was not only *when* I would come along to a rehearsal, but whether I even wanted to, although, in the face of such enthusiasm ('We need all the altos we can get') I did not voice this predicament. Promising to be in touch soon with a date, we left, rather pleased with these people who were so into music, and lived such busy lives, having only lived here just over a year longer than us.

I prevaricated over setting an actual date to attend a rehearsal, because, I suppose, I was still in a blue funk about living in a country I would never have chosen, and culture shock was a contributory factor. Andrew kept phoning, and I kept stalling. In the end, he asked me outright, 'When can we expect you to come out of this self-imposed purdah, then?'

He had me there, and I had to, metaphorically, hold up my hands in surrender to the gun he had suddenly pointed at my head, and I named a date towards the end of the month. Not only did I feel this was a brave thing to do personally, but it was also a move that would cost membership fees, and the purchase of music. The two together didn't add up to a large amount, but things were so tight for us in the purse department that I lost some sleep just worrying about spending those few euros.

Ian told me not to be so silly. We did have some money in the bank, and our house was still to sell. The choir would give me an outside interest and help me meet people (that was one of the things I was afraid of) and I really ought to go. So that was that!

I no longer had a car, so I had to find a way of getting to rehearsals, which were held about fourteen kilometres away, three weeks a month, and a good deal further away once a month. Andrew and June had offered to drive me, if Ian would drop me off at their house first, whence he could collect me when we arrived back. I hated the thought of presuming on other people's kindness like this, but, without a vehicle of my own (and there was no way I was going to drive Ian's huge estate car on what I considered to be the wrong side of the road) there was no other solution.

Besides, Ian, having carefully budgeted for every aspect of our new lives, had decided that there was only the small amount of forty euros a month available to us for fuel, so we had to watch every mile we drove, and not make unnecessary journeys. In the light of that, it would save a small amount of fuel for more mundane but necessary tasks – like going to the tip with the amazing amount of packing material that moving generates, when everything has been unpacked and put away.

And so, one evening, I was duly dropped at their door, for my first evening of choral singing in this far and distant land. (I know it's not far away, but when you're stuck there with no means of escape, it might as well be the very ends of the earth!) This, after all, was not my dream. It was Ian's. This was more my nightmare. Can you feel a slight air of reluctance for the whole plan remaining here? I hope so, for I felt a bit like a bird in a cage, and it wasn't even gilded, it was rusted. And, what's more, my little mirror was busted and I had no bell to play with!

With my warden escorts I arrived at the practice hall for my first dose of serious socialising. Once there, I discovered a close-knit bunch of people who all gathered in their little cliques and chattered. Most of them were English, with only a smattering of French. Nobody really greeted me as a new face in their midst, and I felt about as popular as a fart in a lift. Everyone was brimming over with conversation and bonhomie, and I wondered if I would ever find a place in this group, or whether I was destined to become a permanent outsider.

Although the heating had been turned on, it had only been turned on very shortly before we had arrived, and it was cold and bleak in there, to my jaundiced eye. (I was not adjusting well to my new life.) I duly paid for a copy of Vivaldi's 'Gloria' and was placed next to June (in case I escaped, I think, but at least we weren't shackled together) and we were off.

Oh, no we weren't. The choir mistress, a fearsome woman in, I guessed, her early sixties, was exhorting us to inhale through our noses, then hold out a hand and exhale slowly, as if blowing a dandelion clock (or a feather, or some other flibbertigibbet thing) on the back of our hands while she counted (very slowly) to see how far we could get. She then requested that we pretend to have a hula hoop – of the plastic variety, not the snack – around our waists and make the appropriate motions to keep it there. Was she out of her mind? Why didn't everyone rush her and put her in a straitjacket?

Next, we were exhorted to inhale while slowly raising our arms until we were stretching to breaking point, then exhale slowly, lowering our arms, as if we were pushing down something very heavy. Next was rotating the shoulders and shaking down the arms to relax our bodies. By now, I was sure I had been taken, by accident, to a lunatic asylum, with me being the only person who had noticed this gross error, but everyone else obeyed as if hypnotised. What the bloody hell had I got myself into?

I left that evening, still accompanied by my warders

and, on arriving home, told Ian that they were all out of their minds, and I was never going back. To make things even worse, although the music was quite simple, the level of sight-reading would have disgraced a grade-one student, many of them, I discovered, had no knowledge whatsoever of reading music. Was this really the best choir in the area, or had I been cynically tricked?

My reaction really showed my level of anxiety, when out of my country of origin, and I would like to report that the choir went from strength to strength. I still sing with them now, and it is one of the joys of my week, as the members have grown in both confidence and competence, but, back then, they terrified me, and I cried as Ian exhorted me to give it another try, and think again after the next rehearsal.

STATUS OF UK HOUSE: Still unsold. First viewer still wants to buy it, but cannot find a new buyer for his own home.

CHAPTER FOUR

Tracteur and *Motobineuse*; Joining the Monday quintet; Stopping the back wall from falling off the house; Meeting the builders

TRACTEUR AND *MOTOBINEUSE*

Although Ian was struggling valiantly with the garden, it really was too much for him with just a spade, a fork, and a petrol mower. It was time to do something about the situation, whatever the outcome for our finances.

With this in mind, we went straight to the DIY and gardening store we had begun to use in town. We knew that this gave discounts on a particular day, and had made a point of getting one of its loyalty cards. To our delight, one of the sit-on mowers was on special offer. It was one of their fairly cheap ones, but as they cost a minimum of fifteen hundred euros, to find it on offer was an absolute blessing.

Cunningly we ordered it and put down a deposit, arranging for it to be paid for in full, the same day the following week, and for delivery to be the day after. That way we were able to give them the deposit from our French bank account, and move sufficient money from our UK one to cover the balance, both transactions completed on the day of the ten per cent discount – another saving. Cunning little *rosbifs*, weren't we?

It was a boon, and really cut the time it took Ian to cut our areas of grass, which were a darned sight bigger than they looked at a casual glance. The next problem was, of course, all that digging, to turn the huge patch of land at the back of the barn into a suitable vegetable and fruit garden, to feed us. He had tried hand-digging and, not only did it take a huge amount of time and effort, but he proved to have a glass back, and was always in pain.

Once again we visited the gardening and DIY establishment, and Tony chose a digging machine that didn't seem too horrendously expensive. Unfortunately, you get what you pay for in life, and this thing was trouble from the moment it was delivered.

Firstly, it would not start and, hearing Ian's desperate attempts to bring it to life, our French neighbour from opposite, M Château, came running over to lend his assistance. Now, M Château speaks no English whatsoever, so we all went into Marcel Marceau mode, as we mimed the problems and possible solutions.

I must give him his due. He tried to start the motor about forty times. He also failed forty times, too, and was left bewildered, and with a very sore arm. Eventually the evil little machine gave in, and roared to life, but there was a problem we hadn't anticipated. When putting the various bits and pieces on to it, there had been a little metal rod which Ian had discarded, as he couldn't think what on earth to do with it.

One thing we have learnt about items bought in France is that the instructions are more likely to appear in Klingon than English, so there is a certain amount of guesswork with anything that needs even the smallest bit of assembly.

He took it to where he wanted to start his turning of the earth (clay) and set it going, only to be dragged the width of the garden, flying behind it in its wake. That was when he discovered all he ever needed to know about 'ploughshares'. The little metal rod was supposed to be attached to the machine, so that when it was at work, the rod would stick into the ground and control its speed and efficiency. After this first F1 trip across the garden, there was nothing to show that the machine had ever crossed the ground.

Adding this vital part to the machine, he tried again: or at least he attempted to try again. The blasted thing had stalled, and he was off on another string-pulling marathon, just to get the engine to turn over. This time, ploughshare in place, it did turn some earth, but not very much, then it decided never to start again, and retired into a terminal huff.

We took it back to the shop, and that's where the trouble really started. 'You've used this machine,' accused one of the assistants. 'You cannot change anything that has been used.'

'Of course I've used it,' cried Ian in despair. 'How would I know it wasn't working, if I'd never used it?'

'Nevertheless, we cannot change it, but we will repair it for you.' Such largesse, and we'd just put a small fortune into their tills with these two expensive pieces of gardening equipment. 'Take it to our sister store on the other side of town and we will get a spare for it, whatever it needs. It was manufactured in Italy.' (!!!)

Three weeks later we visited the shop again to ask what had happened to our sad little digger, only to be told that they were still waiting for the part. What method were they using to fetch it? Perhaps a man had set off three weeks ago on a bicycle, and was at this very moment pedalling away, head down, through the Alps, on his way back to south-western France.

Two weeks later we were informed that the new part had been fitted, and that it now worked. Good! We set off to collect it with high hopes, and the man from the maintenance shop took it outside and thoughtfully ploughed up some of the grass verge, to show us how it was now a functioning machine. We brought it home, full of hopes for its use in establishing our vegetable garden.

The next day, Ian dragged it out to the back of the barn and switched it on, and the engine turned over on the first pull. Bingo! Lovely turned earth would be ours, baby plants, for the planting of. After one trip across the garden, smoke began to pour out of it, and Ian had to switch it off in rather more of a hurry than he had switched it on.

Back to the maintenance shop we travelled, this time to be told that it was a new problem but, fortunately, it was only a matter of adjustment, and not another part from Italy. I bet the little old man with the bicycle was relieved to hear this.

Home we went. Back to the back of the barn. Turned on the engine, and the machine began to resemble a bonfire. Sigh! This was really the end. We had coped as best we could with our broken French and the assistants of the two establishments' broken English, but this was war. The thing simply wasn't fit for purpose. It was time to bring a native speaker into the equation, as we simply weren't up to the abuse and contumely needed for this sort of conversation.

Enter Linda, wife of one of the tenors from the choir – annoyed by life in general at the moment, and spoiling for a fight – in exactly the right mood. Ian and she made yet another trip into town, this time to the branch from which we had purchased the machine. 'But you've used it!'

'I know I've used it! And it's already been in for repair twice!'

'But we can't replace it if you've used it!'

'£*%$&*>+*!'

'Ooh la la! Perhaps Monsieur would like to change it for a different model?'

Monsieur did, and one that cost seven hundred euros extra, but at least it was up to the job! What use is a tool that doesn't function? We had got what we paid for, and what we had originally paid for was trash. Now Ian could actually get on with the job of providing a nicely turned over patch of ground in which to plant my precious grown-from-seed babies.

JOINING THE MONDAY QUINTET

Andrew was still nagging me to do something instrumental, so eventually I capitulated, chose the flute as my preferred instrument, and agreed to go along with him to another ex-pat's house, and play music at five o'clock on Mondays.

Andrew and I were to play the flute, our hostess was to be the keyboard accompanist, and a French lady would play the cello, her daughter, the violin. It should be lovely and relaxing. The fact that it wasn't shouldn't have surprised me one little bit, considering how things were going since we'd moved to this heathen country.

Everything we played had to be baroque, and all at about grade eight level. The other four had played through many of the pieces in the past, and were familiar with them. I wasn't, and proved to be the only one sight-reading! It was just like joining the village band back in the UK all over again. The sessions were a battle from start to finish, lasting two hours, and leaving me feeling like a wrung-out dish-rag.

They were fun in a savage sort of way, but after a couple of months, they just stopped. I presumed that I had been politely dropped because I couldn't keep up with the others, and it was only recently that I found out that our hostess and Andrew had fallen out, and the whole thing had been cancelled, and not just me.

I didn't realise that people of that age and maturity could squabble and fall out like tired toddlers, and it still surprises me. I have no time for quarrels, resentment or grudges. Life is just too short for anything other than having a damned good time and living each day as if it were your last. One day you will be right, and it would be awful to die with regrets.

STOPPING THE BACK WALL FROM FALLING OFF THE HOUSE

When we had first viewed the house, we noticed that the west wall at the southern end, which was just wattle and daub, was angled quite steeply at the top, towards the house that sits on the back of ours. The shared wall, we discovered, was being pulled away from our house by the fact that the adjoining roof was tied in with ours halfway down, and was doing its best to become detached.

The owner, not speaking English, but understanding perfectly well what was making us look concerned, immediately ran across the road to the *Mairie* and fetched the mayor to speak to us, rather than lose a couple of 'live ones', which was what we were at the time.

The mayor, with mime, signs, French and minimal English, gave us to understand that the house on the back of what we wanted to be ours was owned by the local commune. It was, therefore, partly the responsibility of the *Mairie* to help to put it right.

We thought this was reasonable, and asked her to get a quote for the work, while putting into our contract of purchase that, should the work exceed a certain sum, we would not complete the purchase. The estimate was duly received, and perceived not to be extortionately high, and we went ahead and bought the place – obviously, or I would not now be writing this.

To date, however, we had heard nothing about the reinforcing of the structure, and enquired when we might have this work done, as the building work on our house would commence shortly. I'd already made an appointment for the chaps we wanted to work on the house to pay us a visit.

To our surprise, a few days later, a man turned up to carry out the work on the wonky wall, did so quickly and efficiently and, to our enormous surprise, the *Mairie* paid the whole bill, not asking us for a centime towards the cost. He also left behind his wooden metre-rule. Result, plus bonus gift!

MEETING THE BUILDERS

I met the first of our builders at the choral society where he sang tenor, and we arranged for him to come round to view the house with his partner, to work out how much what we wanted done was going to cost us. We didn't want to take on anything too specialised ourselves because we wanted it to look right, and not as if we had tackled it as rank amateurs, with no experience or expertise. There's nothing worse than a really bad job of floor-tiling when you have to express an opinion, and the owners of said floor proudly tell you that they laid it themselves.

The choir tenor – husband of Linda – was Beeny, a quiet, reserved man with a beard and occasional glasses, who reminded me, in an indefinable way, of my father. The partner he brought with him, however, was a completely different kettle of fish. To me, he seemed to be massively tall and muscular, with skin tanned like leather and, when he peeled off his woolly hat, a head shaven bare, and as brown as the rest of him. To be honest, he terrified me, and if I'd met him in a dark alley, I'd probably have peed myself, without him having to say a word or do anything.

As they wandered round the wreck of our dwelling, I remembered a make-up bag I had found in my mother's bedroom after she'd died, which turned out to contain just about every set of false teeth she'd ever worn. If only I'd kept them, I could have handed them out so that they could suck someone else's teeth, as they inspected the dereliction.

We knew we needed a bathroom downstairs, and the obvious place was in the disgusting little cubby-hole under the stairs where the lavatory was at present situated. It didn't look like a very big space, but then every corner of this house was proving to be bigger than expected.

We also desperately needed an uprated power supply, and some lighting and power points to keep it company, and Beeny offered to send round a French electrician, whom he knew from other jobs, and get him to do an estimate for us. Not to worry, he reassured us, he does speak a little English. We would wait for that one in trepidation.

The big upstairs space was the biggest priority, being a barn and not fit for human habitation. It needed new floorboards, wiring, dry-lining and ceilings – in fact the whole nine yards. I knew what I wanted it to look like, but my corner took some fighting, or, as the others probably saw it, some heated discussion, but I was adamant.

When that area was finished, I wanted to go upstairs and straight into a large library with a big table in the middle of it, so that if one were browsing, one could lay out as many books as one wanted, and not feel crowded for space.

Our bedroom must lead off from the library, with plenty of space to move around, and not a poky little box where one had to sidle past the bed to get to something else. A very large en-suite would lead from this bedroom, and would be themed to have his and hers ends.

This bathroom was to have a double steam/shower cubicle at the far end for Ian, and a Jacuzzi bath at the window end, for me. In the centre there would be a unit with two large sinks inset, with wall lights to either side, to complement the recessed ceiling lights, and a huge mirror above. At either end of this, there were to be two lavatories – one for each of us. Don't mock. It really works well, and we've had many a cosy chat round the pine sideboard that we adapted to hold the wash hand basins.

How difficult it is to explain that this is a situation

that's an absolute must. In our previous house, if one of us was in the en-suite, the other could just go next door and use the family bathroom. Here, the nearest 'facility' would be all the way through the library and downstairs, and it was singular. It could not be allowed to happen. Two adults fighting over who should use the only lavatory first was simply not on the cards.

Have you ever tried to explain the almost pin-point synchronicity of your bowels with your partner's and not earned a look that said you were one crazy lady, and no mistake – maybe even a bit of a pervert? But each to his own, and this would suit us perfectly as, after nearly forty years together, there are no embarrassing situations left to happen.

One just gets on with what one needs to do on retirement to bed, and one either chats or reads a book. Let's face it; we'd managed with a potty each side of the bed since we'd got here. Why should having something a little more acceptable to squat on make any difference?

In the proposed library, where the stairs came up from the hall, there would need to be some sort of defence to stop anyone having a bad fall off the unprotected edge, and we finally settled for a half-wall which didn't steal any light, and would leave the place looking more open.

The library, we had planned, would have a vaulted ceiling, but this would prove not only to be ugly, with the state of the timbers which, although basically sound, were not pretty, but also probably too wildly expensive.

We were now resigned to having to reduce the price of our UK home again, to get any prospective buyers, and so resources would definitely be much more limited than we had anticipated when we had first planned this devilish adventure.

We had already abandoned the idea of having central heating, and that of replacing the five windows in the property that were very old, thin, single-glazing. Several other refinements went the same way, swallowed and drowned in the belly of a financial depression that would hold sway for years to come. Actually, as I write this now, I wonder when it will all end, as it seemed to start with us putting our UK house on the market in 2007, and hasn't let up yet.

But, back to the builders. They sucked their teeth, then each other's, resisting the temptation to ask if they could have a go with ours too, made joshing little comments like 'God, there's a lot to do', 'Won't come cheap', 'and 'Going to be here some time', while we chewed our nails right up to the elbows and wondered if we should start planning a bank job.

Finally they departed, in grand form, and left us behind to contemplate what the final figure would be, and what we'd have to sacrifice just to get this place liveable, let alone stylish. The answer, when it came, was 'not as much as we thought', and it would just take the sale of our other house to 'let loose the dogs of building' in our encampment.

The French electrician, Dom, arrived about two weeks later, boomed his way around the property – his voice had a particularly resonant quality which I would get used to being awakened by, every Saturday morning, for what seemed like an eternity – then left to decide how much he would charge us for his services, if we didn't mind him fitting us in at the weekends, as he had a day job, and was only trying out being self-employed.

STATUS OF UK HOUSE: First viewer STILL wants to buy it, but the chances of a buyer being found for his own property are slipping away by the day.

CHAPTER FIVE

Old friends again; A run-in with the natives; New friends; Some pitfalls in learning the lingo; Disaster; Marbles meets his first chicken

OLD FRIENDS AGAIN

True to their word, Kay and Robert, who had visited in January flew out again to visit, help again with the garden, and look at more properties themselves, with a view to moving somewhere very nearby. We had discussed all sorts of possibilities for money-making schemes, and decided that we would definitely go into business together setting up Internet marketing sites, Ian and Robert with hand-made wooden toys, Kay and I with arts and crafts. How naïve we were in those early days.

So they moved back into their old room, through which we had to traipse to reach our bedroom, one potty per room, and again contacted the local estate agent that they had liaised with on their last visit.

She must have dredged up every weird, unsalable, and unsuitable property on her books *again*, and we found ourselves looking at wrecks that had no inside staircase, properties, the land belonging to which was at a distance, or interrupted with tiny parcels of land belonging to family members other than those who were marketing the property.

We looked at one house that had only a very uneven and rock-hard earthen floor on the ground floor rising about two feet between front and back, others that had so many derelict buildings on the land that it would cost a fortune demolishing them just for safety's sake, before anything could be spent renovating the main property that was for sale.

Eventually, we asked the estate agent to call round to our modest wreck, so that she could assess what they required in size, although they wanted considerably more land than we had, and also to give her an idea of a state of dereliction beyond which they were not prepared to go. The woman looked around our very humble abode in bemusement, and summed up her feelings by saying, 'There aren't a lot of places like this left.' They were evidently out of stock!

One property we had driven a considerable distance to view simply took the biscuit. The agent showing us round was a young man who met us there, and led us into a courtyard in which an 'L' of a building stood. The courtyard was lumpy, strewn with detritus and uncared for, and it looked as if no one had lived there for some considerable time.

First, we viewed the outside, looking through windows here and there just to see how much light there was in the rooms, and an inspection through one window rewarded us with a sight that could have represented Napoleon's nursery, for it contained a crib that must have been home-made about two hundred years before, draped and connected to other parts of the room and its sticks of crumbling furniture with thick ropes of cobwebs.

Eventually we decided to look at the interior, and the agent had a grand fight with a large bunch of keys, trying to select the correct one to open the door in the right-hand arm of the 'L'. He never located it, and he was ordered to return to his office and not come back until he had the right equipment to open up this ruin for our inspection.

While he did this we gave the exterior a pretty good going over visually. Looking through a filthy window, we saw that not only was the place in a deplorable state of neglect and damp and probably without any electricity or indoor plumbing, but it seemed to end at the corner of the 'L'.

This didn't faze the young man at all when he returned. He simply led us back across the courtyard, approached the other leg of the 'L' and began his search for the correct key to this particular front door. This was the part of the house with Napoleon's crib in it and, like the other section, had a low doorway and very low ceilings. There didn't seem to be any stairs in either section, when we got to enter by the other door, but the two parts were divided by this mysterious square in the corner of the property. From the lack of stairs, we deduced that the first floor must be undeveloped, rather like our large upstairs, back in Saint-Sylvain.

Having admired the two-hundred-year-old collection of dirt and detritus, it was time to ask questions. Were there actually any stairs that we had, perhaps, overlooked? No. Were we correct in thinking that the two halves of the property didn't connect in any way? Yes. Why was this so? HOW was this so?

Apparently a previous owner had sold off the square that formed the part of the dwelling where the two lengths joined, and it was now a garage belonging to someone else, with the door round the other side, invisible from this courtyard. The mystery was explained, but made a house it would be impossible to live in in wet weather. It was like two separate dwellings, neither of which was big enough to live in.

Exasperation began to set in as we questioned him further. Where was the land? Oh, not that bit at the front of the property, but way down on the other side of the barn. The barn that was closest to the house and built of stone? No, the semi-derelict barn that seemed to consist of a glorious collection of rusting corrugated iron and old timbers. The nice barn belonged to someone else. Did the young man have the key to this particular barn? No. Why not? Don't know. Then will young man kindly arrange for the key to be delivered and furnish us with a peek, forthwith.

We knew we were wasting his time now, but it was a conscious act to gain revenge on the agency for sending us to such a ridiculously uninhabitable house. The only way to gain something liveable out of the mess would be to buy back the garage – unlikely – demolish the whole bang-shoot and start again. It wasn't a house at all. It was a building plot with an expensive 'to demolish' hovel on it.

So, we soldiered on to a property that had only a hundred and fifty square metres of land, when Kay and Robert had specified at least – at the very least – ten times that much, preferably a couple of hectares. Kay, being a very polite woman, duly admired the flower beds and tiny rockeries while, inside, I could see she was boiling with rage. Why did no one ever listen to clients' requirements, then note them down accordingly? This time, it appeared that the details had a typing error on the amount of land available, some thoughtless person having typed an extra nought on the area of garden.

The next visit was to leave all four of us depressed and down in the dumps. It was a fairly modern build with a fabulous view. The current owner had bought it as his dream house, and had started work on it with gusto, extending, modernising and replacing windows and doors. Unfortunately his relationship with his partner had broken up and he had also run out of money, which was a common problem in 2008.

Evidence of his unfinished handiwork was everywhere. A cement mixer, unfitted cupboards and windows, tools, bags of cement, tiles and bags of adhesive. The whole place reeked of despair, with a thick layer of dust over everything. None of us could stand the atmosphere, and we left as quickly as possible. To discuss moving on the work and actually living there seemed as devastating as desecrating a grave.

They were game enough to make offers on a couple of properties they visited, but very much lower than the ridiculous asking prices and were, inevitably, turned down. From one agent on our travels, however, we did hear a very amusing story – no doubt apocryphal.

Most of the properties with land that the four of us looked at were owned by whole tribes of children after the parents had died, that being the law here. There's no point in trying to leave all your ill-gotten gains to the RSPCA, for the law insists that the property is divided up between your offspring.

This story involved the viewing by a couple of a semi-derelict house becoming more and more disheartened as they were shown round. They finally came to a bathroom which was absolutely immaculate, and fitted with a modern bathroom suite.

'But this is lovely,' exclaimed the prospective buyer.

'Oh I'm terribly sorry, sir, but this room is not for sale. It belongs to the youngest son.'

'You mean he'll still own it after the house and land are sold?'

'I'm afraid so, sir.'

'And continue to use it?'

'I should imagine so.'

It may sound mad, but a lot of the properties over here are rather like that, and their sale is problematic, to say the least, as a whole gang of siblings must agree to the offered price. I don't know about anyone else's family for sure, but my lot fought like cat and dog at the first opportunity, sibling rivalry being alive and well and a guest at any of our get-togethers.

Nothing even vaguely suitable was found during their second stay with us, and our friendship suffered as well from being at such close quarters. It is not easy to sleep in a bedroom when you are only the thickness of a door and a thin dividing wall apart. Pre-sleep conversation that usually unwinds one after the cares of the day became almost impossible, and, one night, we managed to have a monumental argument conducted just in silence, with the odd hiss thrown in for emphasis.

One of the reasons there was such tension, was that Kay knew so much about gardening, and had a natural tendency to take over jobs that she thought she could do more quickly than a rank beginner – usually me – or would just do things without asking if she knew we wanted it done. Me, being a confrontational maverick and control freak, found I just couldn't put up with that. This was *our* garden, not a practice one for her, and I resented everything she planted. The babies were my job: the only one I had undertaken in relation to growing our own food, and I was very sensitive about it.

This was one job I *could* do and, what's more, enjoyed doing. I called it 'making my babies', and any interference in it resulted in a high-class tantrum from me. I hid it well, though, and Kay never knew. I just refused to plant the seedlings when they came up, and cocked them a snook, leaving them for Ian to deal with. I wanted nothing to do with the little bastards. It's lucky I have never tried living in a commune. I wouldn't have made much of a success of it.

A RUN-IN WITH THE NATIVES

At about this time, we realised that there were great disadvantages to living so close to the *salle des fêtes* (village hall). While it was an advantage that it was no distance to go if there was a commune event on there during the day, the night was a completely different kettle of fish. If someone hired it for a private party, there were no time restrictions on when that party had to end and local disruption cease. We knew that both our English and French neighbours had complained to the mayor, but we had not done so, so far.

As we were still sleeping in the north part of the house, with our very thin single-glazing, we were particularly affected one night, when the weather had turned pleasant. As smoking in any public place has been banned in France as well as England and other European countries, the only way that party-goers could indulge in their habit was to go outside and, boy, do the French like to smoke.

The noise proved unacceptable when the night was balmy and pleasant, meaning all the windows and doors were flung open, not only to let in some much-needed fresh air, but so that those who wished to light up didn't miss out on any of the fun. After midnight, the music gradually grew louder and louder, as inhibitions evaporated and spirits rose (as well as being consumed).

Lying in our bed of suffering nearby, we were completely exasperated by half past three, and the skin of my teeth finally lost its grip on the end of my tether. I have lost it badly with night-time drunks before and, at one period, we lived for a while on a crossroads where the last dregs used to congregate after chucking-out time on a Friday and Saturday night.

One night, when they were still booming inane rat-arsed conversation after midnight, which was echoing round the four clumps of surrounding houses, I leapt from the bed, opened the window nearest the road and yelled, 'Why don't you shut up and go home?' Ian was horrified in case they came on to our property and vandalised it. They must either have passed the belligerent stage or not reached it, because silence fell abruptly, and the group dispersed without another word. Result! Lucky one!

The noise had reached the same state of being really intolerable and, throwing on my dressing gown and clutching my hot water bottle (our room faced north and was still cold, despite the clement weather), I rushed down the stairs and out through the door. I could not put up with the row any longer and decided I would shut them up if it was the last thing I did.

I approached the first party-goer I saw and asked as politely as I could, in my limited French, if they would turn the music down a little, as we were trying to sleep, just two buildings away. That was when I got it, full-on, from a Frenchman who was obviously not an Anglophile.

The father of the young woman for whom the party was being thrown toddled across in my direction spouting a stream of angry-sounding French. Now, even with my small vocabulary, I knew exactly what he was saying. I think his state of drunkenness had reduced his vocabulary, and it was very simple language he called on, to inform me that I had no right to have an opinion on anything. I wasn't from round here. I wasn't even from France. Why didn't I just shut up and go away? He had a right to do whatever he liked in the country HE was BORN in.

Whenever I don't have sufficient knowledge or the means to deal with an unpleasant situation, I immediately burst into tears. That way, whoever sees what is going on will instantly side with me, as I am the one who is upset. So it was in this case, too. The birthday girl came out of the hall to see what was happening just after he started his harangue.

Having heard what he had yelled, and seen the condition I was in (hurrah for Am Dram skills), she mustered all the English she knew, and apologised profusely, not only for disturbing us until so late, but also for her father's appalling manners. I sobbed my way back to the house (teehee!) and the doors and windows of the hall were immediately closed, allowing us, at last, to get some sleep.

We didn't complain to the mayor on that occasion either, but maybe someone else did, for the noise has never gone on so long or so loudly since, and anyway we don't give a fig, for now we sleep at the south end of the house, behind double-glazing, and any high-octane celebration is just a distant hum to us.

LET THE PLANTING BEGIN

Having dug the ground, Ian was ready to start planting the seedlings and other miscellaneous seeds. Bear in mind that neither of us had any experience of veg production (I'm not including the three-foot-tall bolted Tom Thumb lettuces of the Sahara that was the summer of 1976) so we were really flying by the seat of our pants.

Ian had spent hours poring over gardening books to try to glean information as to what to do and when. Just to add to the confusion, he had been told by somebody local that he should plant by the phases of the moon. While he scoffed at this, we did notice a flurry of activity in the area when there was a full moon, even as far as tractors working deep into the night.

I had planted numerous items in the cold frames, including tomatoes, cucumbers, courgettes, gherkins, various types of squash (which we had no idea what to do with), melons, peppers, and chillies (which I hate). Ian also had seed for carrots, beetroot, parsnips, swedes, turnips, green and yellow beans, peas, sweet corn and strawberry plants. So it was a massive planting exercise.

Now, directly next to our garden was the considerable vegetable garden of our neighbours, Monsieur and Madame Augis, who were farmers. They kept cows, pigs, and chickens and farmed a lot of the land in the area. The vegetables were looked after by the mother of the family who must have been eighty if she was a day. When Ian had first cleared the garden she was delighted as all that massive stock of weed seeds was removed from next to her garden. What was so astonishing was how hard and long she worked in the garden, which was full of healthy vegetables, and this became something of a driver for Ian's efforts and probably kept him in the garden longer to try to outlast the old lady next door. I do remember, however, when he had spent many a long back-breaking hour initially cutting and removing the turfs and cultivating eight twenty-by-three metre beds, him coming in saying how jealous he was of the old lady next door when her son turned up with the tractor and ploughed her whole vegetable bed in about half an hour!

He was getting on well with Madam Augis, passing pleasantries every day across the garden fence, until one day when she appeared and seemed to blank him; it was a while before he realised that it was because that day he was working without a shirt! This really is an old-fashioned place.

The planting took some time, but what a joy to look over that former wasteland and see all that stuff growing. We were starting to realise the dream.

NEW FRIENDS

As the weather began to warm, and spring arrived, we received an invitation, via Paul and Denise, for *apéros* at a house just outside the hamlet, the owners of which were German, and visited about four times a year, every year. Their names, we discovered, were Ellen and Gerhard, and we were summoned for Friday evening at seven sharp.

Now, forgive me for being a little apprehensive, but this area was a pain in the arse to the Germans during the Second World War, and our house was used for the Resistance and for hiding British airmen – very *'Allo 'Allo*! These modern Germans, however, had ignored anything that might impinge on the here-and-now from the past, and had bought a holiday home outside the hamlet in a very isolated position. Paul told us that they had already been burgled four times; once, when every stick of their possessions was removed, nobody local had called the police for a week.

Already I admired their spirit, but I had had no personal contact with anyone German since my pen-pal, when I was about thirteen years old. I was already drowning in French people, still finding it hard to adapt to not having the sound of English voices around me when I went out.

The weather was still chilly in the evenings, so Ian made up the fire, banking it up with logs that would keep it going for some time. We didn't expect to get back any later than nine o'clock, after all. Paul and Denise didn't know the couple well, we didn't know either the couple, or them, well. It could be a very stilted evening, and I can't say I was really looking forward to it, more wanting to get it over with, get home and go to bed to read.

The four of us walked down to their house together, knocking on the door at exactly seven o'clock – the church bells in the hamlet were chiming the hour as our first knock struck. We had both brought contributions of bottles of wine, we duly handed them over to our host, and were ushered into their abode, with me wishing them *Guten Abend*, from the limited German I could muster from my schooldays.

Drinks were immediately distributed, and Ellen came in from the kitchen with a huge bowl of meatballs and a plate of cut French bread. We had expected only the usual peanuts, crisps, and olives, and had, all four of us, already eaten. Ellen was intent on seeing that we didn't die of starvation during the evening, and the food kept coming. So did the wine, and what had started as a rather stilted evening soon descended into one that, interestingly, involved three languages.

I tried everything I could in German just for the fun of it. I had only used it in a practical way when purchasing a handbag in Hamburg when on a cruise, and found that I rather liked being able to put in the odd few words here and there. More food arrived and more wine flowed, and Ian and I were well into things, when I noticed that Paul, in particular, was rather quiet, and I resolved to ask him afterwards what had made him hold back so.

Eventually we all left, rather well-oiled, and started to head for the hamlet. Fortunately Paul and Denise had been up this way before, and had sensibly brought torches, for there is no street lighting whatsoever, nor footpath, between Gerhard and Ellen's house and the little church square in which we four lived.

It was a milder night than we had expected, and the moonlight shone across the surrounding fields and through the still fairly bare branches of the trees, silvering the road with its light, and creating an atmosphere that seemed to declare that we could have been having this nocturnal stroll in any one of several centuries. There were no signs of the modern world anywhere, and only the rustlings of small animals in the ditches at the sides of the road, and the lonely hooting of owls, kept us company, as we wended our somewhat unsteady way home.

In a hushed voice, I asked Paul about his reticence, and he confided that he hadn't really known what to say, as he kept thinking of his father, who had been in a concentration camp in the town in which Gerhard had been born, and who had later died of the injuries inflicted upon him after being shot during his capture. Nuff said!

When we got back to the house, the fire had burnt away completely, and it was with a profound feeling of disbelief that we looked at the clock above the mantelpiece and noted that it was a quarter to one in the morning. Well, that had gone off much better than we had dared to hope, and from that evening forward, we have remained firm friends with Gerhard and Ellen, keeping in touch via e-mail, telephone and Skype between their visits here.

Long after our first evening together, when Ellen and

Gerhard were spending an evening at our house, I plucked up the courage to mention the amount of wine the six of us had drunk that evening, suggesting that it must have been eight bottles. Gerhard, with typical German efficiency and accuracy replied, with a little smile, 'Nein! Nine!' Who says the Germans have no sense of humour?

Paul and Denise were not only the catalyst for our meeting Gerhard and Ellen, but also for meeting other French neighbours. Shortly after we had spent the evening at the Germans' house, we received an invitation, with them, to go for *un apéro à dix-huit heures* – a snifter at six.

Accordingly we got out of our work-filthy clothes, cleaned the grime off ourselves, and dressed in appropriately grown-up clothing for visiting. On arrival and after introductions, Denise explained that Pascale spoke only a few words of English and Gerard absolutely none. It was up to us.

Pascale is a PE teacher who was as slim as a rasher of bacon, and has wild hair in natural ginger corkscrew curls which made her look very like an untrimmed poodle, as she also boasted a particularly long snout. Gerard was the archetypal Frenchman, not too tall, but slim, with a neat haircut, the obligatory moustache, and twinkling eyes. He had been a *pompier* – or fireman, before he retired at a fairly young age. Two years previously he had lost the top of one of his fingers in a misunderstanding with an electric plane, and was still wearing a fingerstall because it gave him so much pain. Possibly because of nerves, I thought it looked quite sinister.

Back to the language, however, and off we went. We dusted off what we could, and I felt quite proud of the fact that I could tell them how long we had been married, and what children we had, with their names and ages. Instead of a house-point, I was upbraided for using the formal *vous* and not the singular and informal *tu*. This was news to me.

In experimental oral French classes when one is only

ten years old, no one says anything about *tu* because the objective was to coach in conversation with adults, not between ourselves. I went home to retrieve a dictionary and was told I could refer to it as *le dico*.

Much hilarity was had from my many attempts to pronounce accurately the French word for 'rust'. Pascale had tears of laughter in her eyes as I tried yet again to get that particular sound which does not exist in English. It was a good evening, despite, or maybe, because of the language barrier, and she declared that between the six of us, we should all use *tu* – a compliment to be given permission so soon into the relationship, but had me running for the hills for a whole new aspect to verbs which I had, hitherto, known nothing about.

Almost hot on the heels of this evening came, via the same source, an invitation to visit a local artist-cum-historian-cum architect-cum-eccentric, one Jean-Marc Rubio, who lived down by the little lake where the do-its lived. His house looked like it was a wood-frame house from yonks ago, but turned out to be a new-build which belonged to the local commune, and which he rented.

He offered us wine outside at an old wooden table in what, he informed us, were eighteenth-century glasses and, when it was time for nibbles, these he also brought outside, serving everything from specialist bread to ewe's cheese with an old clasp knife straight on to the surface of the table.

He is a tall, very thin man with hair that flopped over his forehead and was wearing what was, visible through his clothes, unmistakably a lace-up corset. We were to learn that he suffered from a back problem but, at the time, it certainly gave us pause for thought. With his slightly eccentric mode of dress, this all added up to making him look rather like a slightly disabled pirate.

The garden piece of land at the front of his house was full of fascinating old things in various states of dilapidation and he explained that, after a rather expensive divorce, he had obtained everything he owned from the *déchetterie* – the local tip. This included the table and even the chairs we sat on, which I now noticed were all of a different design and era.

He spoke not one word of English, but was very hospitable and talkative. After a while I sort of got my ear in with him, but the Nottingham accent of Denise kept clouding my comprehension. He talked of cinema, of history, or art, and showed us some of the exquisite items he had made. He also told us that, when he was young, it had been decided that he was not talking because his tongue was too long, so his parent had arranged an operation to shorten it. Henceforth he had never tried to learn a foreign language. What a unique excuse!

I did get one peek into the interior of his home, when I went to see where he had got to after a long absence. It was stacked floor to ceiling with other items that looked as if they had the same provenance as his outside furniture. Hurriedly, he hooshed me out, and left me pondering the mystery of how he managed to find enough space for him to even live inside. I am still none the wiser, though he has sat in our garden with us many times chatting and sipping, and dated pieces of provincial furniture which I have picked up. I seem to have an eye not only for a bargain, but for Napoleon III!

SOME PITFALLS IN LEARNING THE LINGO

Ian and I had been studying French at home with various courses we had bought (and not managed to find the time to work with) before our arrival, and having several sets of French neighbours certainly helped guide our faltering tongues, as none of the native neighbours spoke English. We coped, with a liberal sprinkling of mime, and the use of a small dictionary, passing it back and forward between whoever we were trying to communicate with, because we had to; and most entertaining it was for a while.

I had only had this experience before when I had taught English as a Foreign Language, and had landed a beginners group consisting of a mixed bag of nationalities. How I missed being able to tote around a small board and some chalk.

These were acceptable solutions to conversation in our own hamlet, but in the wider world, it caused some fine mix-ups, and I shall never forget the most embarrassing of them all. I had needed to take some antibiotics for a chest infection I had developed, and the inevitable result was that I had a fine dose of candida; or thrush, as it is commonly known in England.

This was not the sort of word to get from neighbours with whom we weren't on intimate terms, so I dutifully searched a dictionary until I found a reference under 'thrush' marked 'med' – medical. Thence, in my head, I composed what I would say in the pharmacy, and thus avoid the embarrassment of having to mime my little problem. One of the other things I didn't know was that, where in England we ask for something 'for' a condition, in France they ask for something 'against' a condition – *contre*.

When I entered the pharmacy there were no other customers, and that suited me very well. I was still somewhat embarrassed at trying out this newly acquired vocabulary, and was pleased to find that I would be doing it without any audience other than the assistant at the counter. Girding my loins, I fired off what I thought meant 'Have you got anything for thrush?'

She goggled at me as if I'd spoken in Swahili. I tried again, and still received nothing but a confused expression, and the calling over of another assistant to see if she could help this strange foreign woman. The next time I asked, I scratched at my arms, miming the itching I was suffering in a much more intimate place.

The second assistant went off to fetch something for general itchiness, as a queue began to build up behind me. Refusing the proffered crème, I repeated my plea, still scratching at myself in mime, and added, '*dans mes culottes*'. Still nothing but puzzlement radiated back at me, and now the little pharmacy was almost full, and I had an appreciative audience for my little performance.

Gritting my teeth, I mimed the whole embarrassing scratching process through my clothes in the appropriate but embarrassing area, as smothered titters came from behind me, but enlightenment dawned. '*Ah! Champignons!*' exclaimed the first assistant, and went to get me the required medication.

It was only afterwards that I worked out the whole sorry tale. My dictionary or my eyesight had let me down, and I had actually gone in there and asked if they had something FOR lily of the valley! – a small vase perhaps, or a pair of scissors to cut them to size?

My next puzzling statement had indicated that I had itching all over my body, and in several pairs of knickers. I'm surprised they didn't put me in a straitjacket, or at least call the gendarmes. And her statement of the single word 'champignons' also gave me the local word for the condition – they call it 'mushrooms' over here.

So, beware! If you accidentally ask for mushrooms in a pharmacy, you will be sold a little tube of cream and a suppository. However, if you find anything growing in your garden that resembles mushrooms, it is perfectly normal to take them into a pharmacy and ask them to identify whether they are poisonous or good to eat.

If you ask for mushrooms in a restaurant, you might enjoy them more, especially if they've been fried in garlic butter.

In fact, just shopping for food had become a major hurdle. Pictures and diagrams on tins are all very well but,

I knew from my experience, as a Greek teacher, that this could not answer all the questions that need to be answered as to their content. I once had a couple sign on for my beginners' course because they had just lugged back, from one of their many trips to Greece, what they had thought were huge tins of olives, for their local pub.

On grand opening day at the bar, they had cut round the vast top of the tin in expectation of oohs and aahs at the delicious plump fruits within, only to be showered with laughter. The olives on the outside were an indication of the source of the oil on the inside. There was not an olive in sight, but enough oil to fry the harvest of a potato farm.

Also, when on holiday there myself, I had often been stopped by English shoppers who, having heard me speaking English to Ian, could see that I was actually reading labels instead of staring at them in mystification, asking what sort of milk they were looking at, and if I could point them at the skimmed version; or could I identify whether this or that package was butter or margarine, and what sort of cheese was in this packaging. Shopping isn't always a walk in the park, and at least, in France, the alphabet is recognisable and, therefore, easier to look up, even if your dictionary is far too small to include any of the words you do not understand!!!

And so we started shopping with a dictionary in tow, evidently far too small, but useful for enigmatic shop signs and also instructions on road signs which were not immediately obvious. We did not yet have a mobile phone that would allow us access to a translation service, and the little dictionary did little to help us, except to inspire us to increase our vocabulary as far as foodstuffs in general were concerned.

Ian's first big muddle-up came when he was ripping out what there was of the wooden division that separated the kitchen area from the shower area, and screened both of them from the rest of the middle room. The work surface also had to be ripped out, as we would be using a number of oak sideboards to form our kitchen cupboards and island. The wood could be put to good use, and Ian sneaked it off to his secret hoard of bits of wood, that all men keep somewhere.

The work surface, however, would have to be dumped, as it was just an old piece of board with ghastly salmon pink and yellow tiles glued to it so strongly that the bond would no doubt last till doomsday, had it persisted in its present form.

'I'll take it down to the *déchetterie*,' he said, showing off the shiny new word he'd learnt for the tip. We had also been looking at the verbs 'to be' and 'to have', and he drove off confident that he could now locate the right area of the tip in which to dump his unwanted lump of junk.

When he returned home, he was very quiet and not a little embarrassed, so I asked him how it had gone. 'I got my *être* mixed up with my *avoir*,' he said, shamefacedly.

'What do you mean?' I asked, still none the wiser.

'Well, I got it all lined up in my head, what I was going to say to find out where to dump that bloody old tiled work surface, but when it came to it, I went up to the man and, instead of "I have," said, "I AM a piece of wood with tiles on!" and he laughed fit to bust.' So did I, dear reader: so did I!

I did a similar thing when a friend of ours moved over here (more of that later – next volume) and I took him to the medical centre to sign on with a doctor. 'Don't worry,' I told him. 'I'll do all the talking, then proceeded to say to the receptionist, 'Here is my English friend who is now living in France, but he ISN'T a doctor,' rather than he hasn't got one. She gave me one of *those* looks that said, 'Damned *Rosbifs* can't sort out their *êtres* from their *avoirs*, and said not a word about my abuse of her mother tongue, merely handing me the appropriate form for him to register.

DISASTER

During this month we reluctantly accepted another offer on our UK house. The original viewer still desperately wanted to buy it, but the possibility of this actually happening was getting more and more distant. It was with reluctance, therefore, that we had asked the agent to carry on marketing it. The original viewer's offer was thirty thousand pounds below our asking price, but he said that he would better the offer if he could, when his property was sold.

We then had a new offer from another buyer, and this one was twenty thousand less than the original, so that made it fifty thousand down on what we had originally hoped to achieve. I could see our refurbishment fund shrinking so much, that there was a danger we wouldn't have any money left at all by the time it finally sold. With every month that passed, we still had to pay the mortgage and council tax (discount for an unoccupied property a miserly ten per cent!), and Ian's pension really was too small for us to live on, what with the disastrous state of the pound against the Euro.

After all, we were supposed to retire here. At some point we were going to have to find another solution to our financial problems. They were not going to go away and, having investigated French law for self-employment, it was an impossibility for us at that moment, as the only way I would be able to work would be to register as a *micro-entreprise*, and that involved a lot of costs during the first two years, to a level that we simply couldn't afford.

Entrepreneur may be a French word, but it doesn't seem to be understood by the French government. What

Revolution? They might as well not have bothered, the way the people trying to better themselves are quashed and demotivated.

There were rumours of a change in the self-employment laws, however, and if these actually came about, it would have made it much easier for me to teach here, without the pile of money I would have needed for the current system. Something needed to happen, because when we bought the house the pound was worth €1.40. When we arrived here, it was worth €1.20. If things went on much longer as they had been, it would soon be at parity, and we might as well have climbed on to the roof and said goodbye to a cruel world.

As if this situation wasn't enough, that day we had a call from the estate agent to say that the new buyer had pulled out of the purchase, and we were left only with the original offer, that was unlikely to come to anything, so it was back to square one for us – not a happy situation at all, and our life here felt like it was balanced on a knife-edge.

MARBLES MEETS HIS FIRST CHICKEN

Not wanting to end my account of this month on such a gloomy note, I remembered Marbles' first run-in with a chicken. The farmers behind us keep cows, pigs and chickens, as well as growing crops. In the field behind our house, the hens run free, picking at all the delicious greenery in the wildness of that piece of land.

The fence between our two properties is a wire one and very ancient. In places it has drooped very low and, one day, Marbles took a little trip over one of these droops to see what he could find on the other side that might be of interest to him.

What he met was a large and rudely healthy chicken, just pecking around and minding its own business. This looked like a good lark to him, so, as I watched, fascinated, he crouched down on his haunches to stalk this interesting new specimen, hoping to add it to his repertoire of 'things I have caught and/or killed'. Slowly, slowly he began his stalk, creeping ever nearer to his target. It had feathers, so it must be a pushover.

Boy, was he surprised when the chicken not only stood up to him, holding out its wings and approaching him, but had no intention whatsoever of rolling over and playing dead. He stopped abruptly and had a little think about it, then tried to look menacing. The chicken matched his display of bravado with one of her own, and started to move slowly towards him.

That was enough for Marbles. This bird definitely hadn't played by the rules, and it looked like, if he didn't take evasive action, he'd have had his chips with this chicken. Yellow streak right down the middle of his back, he turned and fled, finally taking refuge in our barn where he thought he'd be safe or, at least, close enough to home to yowl loud enough to summon someone to his rescue. No more chicken monsters for Marbles. He may be a huge cat, but that hen seemed to be able to grow at will. He'd stick to smaller prey in the future; prey that didn't look as if it might engage in battle and leave him the loser.

STATUS OF UK HOUSE: Original viewer STILL wants to proceed with purchase but has no buyer. Subsequent offer by another buyer has been withdrawn. We are still on the market, and losing hope that it will ever sell.

CHAPTER SIX

Lizards and other pests; Monkey does VE Day; Lucy; Francis and partner

LIZARDS AND OTHER PESTS

Lizards have come to dominate our lives. Never having come across them before in their previous lives in the UK, the cats are fascinated with these little clockwork toys that work for quite a long time before they break. We were finding them everywhere, either intact, without a tail or, even, without a body – just a lone head lying on the floor, still staring in disbelief at its cruel end.

Leaving the house, even for such a short time as for shopping, brings a bundle of surprises when we return. Walking in with arms full of bags is not an option, as one is likely to step on a dead lizard, or a part thereof.

It had been mice and rats before, but they seem to have exhausted the supply in our barn, Paul and Denise's barn, and any of the other barns in our little locale. Now it's warmer, lizards are all the go, and they don't just come in one size. Some of them are anything but dinky.

Monkey came in one day recently with what looked like a brightly coloured plastic green and yellow dinosaur toy wrapped around her head and neck. This, on inspection, proved to be a rather larger variety of lizard, and we weren't sure who had captured whom. Although she seemed to have her teeth into the body of this creature, it had its feet and tail wrapped firmly round her neck, and looked as if it was attempting to squeeze the life out of her.

Ian would do nothing until he had on a pair of stout

gauntlets. With the smaller lizards here, the children put them on to their tongues, to get them to bite, and see how long the little creatures can hang on for.

It took him quite a tussle to get the two of them disentangled, and his first move was towards an open window to dispose of the thing outside. It gave us both the willies, but she was the only one of the cats that had the guts (or maybe the stupidity) to tangle with them. If either of us saw one in the garden, we left it alone, with the exception of one that we discovered outside the front door on the drive, injured.

It looked such a pathetic thing, with a big tear in its skin, lying there out in the open sun with no protection from predators, so I asked Ian if he would put it somewhere safe, possibly on the little wall just outside the fence that fronted our property. Huffing off in search of the gauntlets again I left him to it and went indoors, forgetting all about it until later, when I asked him if he'd moved it to a safer place.

'Well, yes and no,' he answered, and pointedly looked in any direction but mine.

'What do you mean, "yes and no"? Either you did or you didn't. Which is it?' I asked, annoyed at not getting a straight answer to a simple straight question. 'Did you put it on the wall like I asked you to?'

'Not quite. I did my best,' he said with a pout.

'So what happened?'

'I couldn't be bothered to go out on to the road, so I thought I'd just lob it over the fence.' He really doesn't like those things. 'Which I did,' he added, 'and it landed on the road.'

'Did it make its way to safety after that?' I asked, wondering if he was worried I'd tell him off for throwing it, when it was already injured.

'Not really,' he answered, and was reluctant to go on.

'Come on! Give!' I pushed him. 'What happened?'

'It got run over by a car,' he replied, then looked surprised when I burst into peals of laughter. It wasn't that I thought the tragedy of the situation was amusing, it was just the thought of Ian stewing all afternoon because he knew he'd have to tell me that he hadn't checked the road for traffic when he let loose his missile. Poor lizard!

MONKEY DOES VE DAY

Our sociable little Abyssinian cat, Monkey, loved to socialise, and often visited the houses of our neighbours, just to check that they were all right, and that nothing interesting had happened to the interiors of their homes while she hadn't been looking.

When May 8th came round, we decided that we would attend the small ceremony at the war memorial which, at that time, was just opposite our dining room window, by the side of the church. Even with something as simple as this, there were lessons to be learnt, here, in the vast expanse of 'abroad'.

The first mistake we made was to cross the road just before 11 a.m., me wearing my father's medals; and waiting and waiting and waiting. No one else turned up, so we went home and took seats in the dining room to see what, if anything, would happen.

Just before twelve o'clock, a small crowd started to assemble and the lady mayor arrived. It had never crossed our minds that, if the ceremony was at eleven o'clock in the UK, it would be at exactly the same time here – one hour ahead, at twelve noon.

Back over we went, while the mayor made a speech, and read out the names of all the war dead listed on the memorial, and after each name there was a muttered phrase from those assembled, which we soon identified as *mort pour la France* – 'died for France', which we too intoned in respect.

There were various floral tributes laid by a number of people, no doubt of importance in the local community, and this is where one of our very own stole the limelight. Many of the crowd took photographs of this laying of the flowers, and Monkey strolled right up to where they were laying them at the foot of the memorial, and sat and posed beautifully, like an Egyptian cat. Within a minute it was her that was being photographed, rather than the floral tributes.

The next stage of the ceremony was to go round the corner to where a headstone had been planted many years ago. This marked the place where a young man from the Resistance had died, shot by a German bullet. He had apparently been targeted after leaving the restaurant that was now our dining room, taken shelter in a neighbour's barn, then made a run for it round the corner, only to be killed before he'd got more than about fifty yards.

Another speech was made and, this time, white lilac was laid in profusion. And who was in the middle of all this scented beauty? Rent-a-celebrity cat, of course, lapping up the attention and the 'oohs and 'aahs that she attracted.

But she hadn't finished her public appearances for that day. After the ceremonies, everybody went into the village hall where drinks and nibbles were waiting for us, so that members of the community who hadn't seen each other for a long time could reacquaint themselves, and new inhabitants could meet some of the old.

In the village hall there is a stage, and I don't think it would take you many guesses to find out who went up on to the stage for an impromptu performance of her grace and beauty. That cat has turned into a right show-off, but when we left, I put her on my shoulder, and she sat there contentedly all the way home, knowing that she had done her all to brighten up the day for the people of Saint Sylvain.

LUCY

Lucy! Oh, Lucy! Oh, no, Lucy! Why Lucy? Why, oh why, had we agreed to our old friend Lucy staying when we would be crammed into two inter-connecting bedrooms, and with her reputation. She had always been Luce by name and Loose by nature. It wasn't that I didn't trust our tiny little community to smother her vanity and her libido, it was just that we'd still like to be speaking to our neighbours when she went back to the UK.

I suppose I eventually crumbled at the story of her latest beau sauntering off with someone younger than her. That was what really did it. Lucy is at exactly the right age for a mid-life crisis, and is terrified of ageing. She would go to any lengths still to look youthful and gorgeous.

Unfortunately she is in her forties, has had her face punctured, as many times as a teabag, with Botox, in an effort to avoid wrinkles, has to eat like a sparrow to retain her figure, and can be quite obsessive about exercise, her highlights, her tan (electric, being English) and false nails. Her clothes are also inappropriately on the young side for her, and she always totters around on the most impossible of heels.

Add that to the fact that she is definitely a party girl, has had more live-in partners than anyone we know, and drinks like a fish. She is a hangover from our early days when we were young and lived a more wild and adventurous life. Unfortunately, because of the number of times she has had to re-invent herself for a new bloke, she has hardly changed, except for becoming a bit more leathery, and definitely more desperate, since this latest breakup.

We, on the other hand, have changed considerably, especially since our move here. Everything has been such physical hard work, dealing with the state of the house as best we could to make it liveable before we (hopefully) get some funds to do some proper work on it, and taming the garden, not to mention all the humping around of all the very heavy furniture we purchased especially for this place.

Whereas her ideal day starts around noon or even 1 p.m., culminates in pouring a few liberal libations down her throat before going out on the town, then staggering into bed, usually stocious (drunk), at 2 or 3 a.m., we now rise reasonably early (I, slightly later than Ian), work like slaves, getting covered in dirt, cobwebs, peat, earth, or *lasure* – a liquid treatment for wood; then we break for lunch and do the same thing all over again in the afternoon.

By the time we get round to the evening meal, it's much earlier than we used to eat and we go for something as simple as possible, just to get some fuel into our depleted bodies. We're ready for bed, some nights, at a ridiculously early hour. When we very first arrived here, we both sat in front of the fire exhausted and hardly able to keep our eyes open at the end of every day, ready for bed whether it was seven o'clock or even half-past, but, as I said to Ian at the time, it is the best evidence of how physically tough life is over here.

I don't think Lucy is going to get on very well with our new routine, and some adjustments will have to be made on both sides, if her visit is to be bearable. My biggest worry, with us being out in the sticks and there being nowhere really for her to vent her exuberance, is that she'll party here, drink us dry and keep us up long after we have metaphorically turned into pumpkins.

If we're lucky, she'll view her stay with us as a time to recuperate after the disappearance of her last beau, and refresh her body for the next round of mate-hunting. We can't even take her for a drink in the evenings, as all the bars in the local town close their doors at 7 p.m., and by that time Lucy hasn't even revved up her engine to make sure she's ready for the fray.

We're due to pick her up from the airport this afternoon, and everything's ready for her: the wine is in the barn. As it's so cheap and plentiful here, and she is no connoisseur, we have purchased a number of five litre 'fat-boys' at five euros a throw, to keep her in red and rose, and some litre cartons of paint-stripping white which, with the addition of a few ice cubes, becomes a libation fit for human consumption. We can't afford to provide her with bottles, but if the wine is poured into a carafe before being offered to her, she'll be happy enough, as her favourite drink between men is always 'the next one'.

We also have a cupboard out there plentifully stacked with large bags of snacks. Lucy may be paranoid about her figure, but when she's had a few, she could snack for England as she suddenly develops hollow legs, then, at the next meal, asks for only very small portions, as she's watching her figure. I sometimes feel like telling her that if she watched her figure when she's on the toot, she might be very surprised at the way it behaves.

At the airport, it's the same old Lucy who flings her arms round my neck and hums with delight at being reunited with her 'bezzie mate' from school. Ian, she has known only a couple of years less than I have, and she repeats this process with him, taking the time and effort to give him a big sloppy (and a little over-prolonged) kiss. We shall have to talk thereon, when we are in private, I decide.

She is definitely on a high on her arrival here and, on the forty-minute car journey back to the house, babbles happily away in the back of the car about how she is so over 'what's-'is-name', should never have trusted him in the first place, and it was only because he reminded her of her first love at school that she ever had anything to do with him at all. Now, she is determined to meet someone with whom she can have a meaningful relationship, and settle down once and for all.

I sit in the passenger seat, silently scoffing. The number of times I have heard this before is beyond count, and I idly wonder if someday it might actually be true. I have a feeling it's not just yet awhile. She's simply got too much energy left to settle down to a normal life, and must get it all out of her system before she can even think of acting like a grown-up.

Her reaction to the house is exactly how I imagined it would be; a mixture of 'OH, my God!' to 'Oh, my GOD!' Yes, she agrees, it's going to be a fantastic house when it's finished. Perhaps she'd better come back then. What, no bathroom? Only a shower cubicle in the kitchen? No wash-hand-basin at all? Only one loo, and that downstairs as well? Dear God! How had we managed to live like this for months?

'You get used to it,' I told her, feeling very defensive about our darling old wreck, and not wanting its feelings hurt, when we loved it so much.

Ian lugged her enormous suitcase upstairs and heaved it on to the bed she would be sleeping in, in the first bedroom at the top of the north staircase. I followed, wondering what on earth she could have found to bring with her for such a quiet break, and stood, looking on with interest, as she unlocked it and flung open the lid.

My eyes nearly popped out of my head as I glimpsed all the hair drying, straightening and curling equipment that one would need to open a small salon. There were also two enormous make-up bags – straining at the zips, they were so full. In one corner of the suitcase were a few wispy wraiths of clothes and satin and lace underwear.

'Lucy!' I almost shouted in astonishment. 'It might be getting warmer in the daytime, but it can be quite cold in the evenings. Have you not brought a jumper or a sweat-shirt? I thought you might at least have brought a pair of jeans.' Then I saw the shoes.

'How on earth are you going to get about the garden in those things?' I asked. 'There can't be a pair of shoes in that case with heels lower than four inches.'

'Garden?' she replied, obviously puzzled. 'I know you've got some decking. Why on earth would I want to explore further than that? If it's sunny I shall lie out there and work on my tan, if not, I shall be inside.' It was all so logical to her. And clear as crystal to me. Lucy was going to be looked after, whether we had planned to pander to her or not.

We ate at home that night, but promised to take her out the following evening. Although there were no bars open in the local town after nursery bedtime, there was a restaurant in a nearby village that boasted a bar, albeit a small one, and we could at least take her there to prove that nightlife, as she knew it, simply didn't exist around here, and she'd better get used to the idea.

After all, she was the one who had extended her proposed stay from four days to a week, so she couldn't hold us responsible if she was bored out of her (one-track) mind. This was how we lived now, and I hoped she didn't take it badly and whine and whinge the whole time she was here about being bored. There was plenty of work to do, all of it dirty, but I somehow didn't see her up a ladder with a paintbrush, in all the 'pulling' outfits she'd brought with her, and there was no way I was having her perched on a ladder in the only alternative, which was naked.

On her second day, I arose unaccustomedly late. She had quaffed wine well into the small hours, telling me what a shit her previous bloke had been, then reviewing what seemed to be every relationship she'd had over the last twenty-five years. Although I only drank one glass of wine to her three, I was wrecked when I awoke the next day, and looked at Ian with envy – he had pleaded exhaustion about ten-thirty, and swanned off to bed – a smug smile on his face at his ingenuity.

We had a scratch meal before we went out, as our purse did not extend to three people eating in a restaurant and we were, after all, only going out for a drink. Just before we were ready to leave, Lucy swanned downstairs as best she could in her vertiginous, teetering heels, dressed as only Lucy can; like a cross between a stripper halfway through her act, and someone about to attend a tarts and vicars party, and she certainly wasn't dressed as a vicar.

'You can't go out dressed like that!' I admonished her, suddenly sounding like my mother had when I rolled over the waistband of my school skirt in an attempt to make it shorter.

'Why ever not?' she asked. 'I usually do.'

'Maybe you do – Ian, stop goggling – but you live in urban England, and this is rural France. You need to think of this as a break set in the nineteen-fifties. Things simply aren't the same over here.' Since when have I behaved like a headmistress? She was definitely bringing out the worst in me.

'Well I haven't got anything else with me. All my stuff's like this,' she stated with a small smile of triumph. Nobody was going to cramp her style if she could help it.

'I shall lend you one of my pashminas,' I stated firmly. 'It'll cover up some of your more radical exposed bits, and keep out the chill of the evening.' I might have thought I'd won the day, but she proved me wrong from the moment we stepped into the bar.

As I grabbed a table, Lucy put her bag down next to mine, removed the pashmina and sashayed over to the bar where Ian was ordering the drinks. Every eye in the place was on her, the male ones with delight and longing, the female ones, of which there were very few, with open hostility and hatred. She was like a magnet to iron filings. The attraction was irresistible.

As Ian came over to the table with a tray, I noticed a proprietorial air about him. He was radiating 'Mine! Mine! Mine!', and got his fair share of hostile looks from the men present. Although it had never happened to us before in the bar, the owner came across with little bowls of things to nibble, and set them before her as if he were making an offering to a goddess. And Lucy was openly flirting with him! Golly! We wouldn't be able to come back here in a hurry, or his wife would spit in our beer.

The bar stayed open that night long after the restaurant was empty, Lucy attracting even more attention when the owner put on some music and she began to dance sexily and languidly in the middle of the floor. It was only when she attempted to get on to a table to dance that I restrained her, and dragged her reluctantly back to the car. If she'd fallen from that table, which was highly probable, as she'd drunk quite a lot, I had no intention whatsoever of spending the wee small hours in casualty, waiting for an almost naked woman to be X-rayed.

Some nights she kept me up late relating her triumphs over the years with the opposite sex, some nights she would stay up crying about the failure of her most recent relationship, and how she had been betrayed. Whichever it was, Ian always made the excuse that he had to get to bed at a reasonable hour, because he had a lot to do in the garden the next day. It was always me who got to babysit her into the early hours, hiding my yawns and wishing she would either go home or find herself a husband, and it made me feel like a heel.

One evening we had our neighbours Paul and Denise over for drinks and nibbles, and a bit of music and a chat. That worked well until about three quarters of the way through the evening, when the wine made her maudlin. A particular song started to play, and that was it for her. We were sitting round the dining table sipping and nibbling, and suddenly she had tears rolling down her face.

I had no idea what to do. I didn't want to break up the evening which had been going so well, nor did I want to embarrass her by bringing anyone's attention to it. She didn't leave us in any doubt about why she was crying though, and slurred her way through the story of how this was 'their song', referring to her recent ex, and it sure killed the party mood. Our neighbours left soon after, looking highly embarrassed.

On one unforgettable day we chanced taking her out to lunch. How much trouble could she get herself into at noon? We chose a very quiet restaurant, and took a table at the end of it, by the window, ordering the *plat du jour* as we didn't have the funds to do anything other than order the set menu.

We were about halfway through the meal when Ian noticed that we were getting very fervent attention from the waiter, even though there were quite a few customers eating now, and I noticed that Lucy was grinning, in the way she does when she knows something that other people don't.

Seeing me look at her, she leaned across towards the two of us and whispered, 'I've gone commando today. I've got no knickers on.'

Before he could think about it, Ian had replied, 'That's good. It'll keep the flies off.' I, however, had put two and two together when she suddenly crossed her legs as the waiter was approaching the table.

'Get the bill, Ian,' I hissed, adding, 'NOW!' when he didn't respond immediately.

'Why?'

'I'll tell you when we get home.' If I'd said anything now, he might have sat there in anticipation of Lucy crossing her legs again, but for his benefit this time.

As he paid the bill I hissed straight into Lucy's ear, 'You've been "winking" at that waiter, haven't you?'

She knew exactly what I meant and didn't even try to deny it. 'Well, there's not much to do round this way, is there?' was her only reply.

When I told Ian about her little leg-crossing routine, that being the reason why we had exited the restaurant so fast, he blanched and merely said, 'We can never eat there again,' which I thought was quite restrained of him, given the way gossip has a way of travelling in the English community, and probably in the French as well.

The last straw was probably when I found her upstairs in the barn, lying on a futon we hadn't found room for in the house, tumbling with a French workman who should have been painting the house down the road. I don't know how she had found him, and didn't care. I wasn't having that going on in our barn. We, after all, had to live here after she'd gone.

It was the longest week of my life, and one I wouldn't repeat whatever the circumstances. My bloodshot baggy eyes and puffy face would right themselves after a few days of clean living, but my liver felt irreversibly older, and I made the decision to have my own carafes, should I ever find myself in similar circumstances again – one for red and one for white: grape juice!

Update: Lucy couldn't believe how out in the boondocks we lived and has not managed to find the time to come back since this first visit. As much as we love you, sweetie, long may it remain so.

Now that we were on our own again, it was time to get back to work and my next job was painting the *séjour* floor. This had to be my job as Ian had 'glass knees' to the point of really not being able to kneel at all without great pain. It's lucky his family isn't Irish: he would never have survived training for the priesthood. Anyway, it was my idea to do it in an attempt to hold it together a bit longer until we could afford to replace it (this turned out to be a lot longer than we had anticipated).

The furniture and boxes that had been dumped in this room were removed to the barn so I could really see what I was up against and the size of the floor made me blanche. There must be smaller football pitches than this! Oh well, no point in complaining, just get on with it.

We had bought some paint from the local DIY store in a rich diarrhoea brown colour and when I started to use it I was immediately aware of the strong odour. While I liked the smell (I am one of those strange people who like the smell of tar, creosote, and petrol), it didn't like me and it was not long before I was having to use my inhaler every time I took a break. I have to say I worked like a dog that day and completed the whole floor and boy did it look better. Ian was suitably impressed and I went to bed that night feeling that that I had made a real difference. We might not have our money yet but our dream had made another small shuffle forward.

Later on that month, fired up by my success with the floor, I also applied a coat of this poo-brown paint to the only barn doors we possessed – the other two entrances standing wide to the weather – and also to what should have been the inside of the shutters, had we been able to close them without them falling off the wall. They didn't look too bad from the road. Smoke and mirrors had triumphed again.

FRANCIS AND PARTNER

Francis was the first of our children to visit us, and arrived with his partner David, a man older than us, but with whom we got on like a house on fire. In our opinion, he was the perfect antidote to Francis's more manic moods, and kept him calm and un-bored in an almost magical manner.

I must admit that when they first got together and came to stay with us in the UK, it was a bit bizarre on the first morning, bringing them early morning tea in bed, but that was the only awkward moment, and we always looked forward, either to staying with them, or having them stay with us.

Francis has a weird sense of humour which is exactly like mine, and on many an occasion the two of us have been convulsed with laughter, to the point of tears, while Ian and David look on, bemused, not understanding why we are so hysterical. I have been known to laugh so much in my number one son's company that I have wet myself, and, after one particularly memorable evening when staying with them, after a meal in a South American restaurant, laughed myself sick after we arrived back at their place and started to have a post-mortem on the evening.

While they were here, there was to be a ceremony for 'raising the pine', to commemorate the election of the mayor – in this case, the re-election of the lady mayor, and a meal was included, free to residents who lived in the wider community of Saint Sylvain. We desperately wanted to go, as this only happens once every six years, and it was an ideal opportunity to meet new people so, as Francis said he wasn't feeling one hundred per cent – probably a surfeit of gin-and-tonic the night before – we said we'd go alone, as it was during the day, then I'd cook a leg of lamb in the evening. We couldn't even persuade David to come with us, as the meal was paella, and he loathes seafood.

We trotted off about ten-thirty, both looking forward keenly to what the rest of the morning and the early afternoon held for us. Hospitable and friendly as usual, the tireless organisers met everyone with glasses of various alcoholic and non-alcoholic beverages and plates of tiny nibbles.

The pine itself was a very tall, recently felled tree,

which was bedecked with French flags and rosettes. A hole had been dug for the base of its trunk, and there were two ropes attached to said trunk, higher up. At the appointed hour, two teams of strong locals took their places at the ropes and began to heave.

Slowly the tree began to rise, but the occasional imbalance between the two teams of rope-haulers made it sway dangerously from side to side, drawing gasps from the crowd. After what seemed like a very long time, it was upright, and made secure until the hole could be filled in, and everyone trooped into the hall for our commune lunch.

There was no stinting on the meal, and it ran to five courses and included wine, coffee and *eau de vie* (evil French hooch!), which was poured over a sugar cube on a spoon, balanced over the cups of coffee. The paella itself was juicy, abundant, and filled with an unexpectedly high number of fat prawns – absolutely delicious.

By the time the meal ended, we were firm friends with all the old boys on our table, having dredged up French we didn't know we knew, and had learnt quite a lot about the history of our house, especially during the Second World War, and there were a lot of nudges and winks from the old gentlemen, as they recalled the high jinks that had gone on, where we now led a thoroughly respectable life, and there were many references to and knowing winks about *les chambres*.

We staggered back to the house at about five o'clock, and I promptly lay down on a rug on the floor and fell asleep. The lamb never got cooked, as we were both absolutely sloshed and, in a fine reversal of roles, our son said it wasn't safe for us to be let out unsupervised, and we should be ashamed of ourselves, coming home in that condition. Sweet revenge! – definitely the last course of the meal.

STATUS OF UK HOUSE: A new offer has been made by the buyer who pulled out recently, but she has reduced her offer by twelve and a half thousand pounds. That leaves the selling price sixty-two and a half thousand pounds less than we originally put it on the market for, but she has us over a barrel, and we must accept, or wait for goodness knows how long for another offer.

CHAPTER SEVEN

Cats and coypu; *Espèce de vache*!; Tragedy; UK – pronounced yuk; Coming back home; The baby grand; The scales of justice are rebalanced; A bit of a do, French style

CATS AND COYPU

Now the good weather is here and the evenings are light, Ian has taken to walking down the road nearly opposite our house to the lake, to watch the coypu in the water. Their calls are easily audible at night, and sounded to me like 'do-it, do-it', so we have named them the 'do-its'. They joined in with the frog serenade in the spring, at least until the lake was drained after a couple of local French residents fell out, but that is not a story to tell at this point, because it was well into the future.

The cats thoroughly approve of this evening saunter, and all four of them accompany Ian each evening, and play in the lake's surroundings while he stands and stares and just enjoys the scenery. As soon as he starts to make his way back home, they all assemble and accompany him home, scampering round his heels in a very touching way. I've never seen cats do this sort of thing before en masse, and it's a delight to know that they want to join him in this activity.

I have been so tired that I haven't accompanied him so far, but I'm determined to do so in the very near future, as the whole scene is charming in the extreme.

Even leaving this a day or two was too long, though, for a couple of days later Ian wakes me up and tells me I have to be very, very brave. My darling silver spot Bengal, Meep, is no more, having been hit by a car in the night, and a neighbour has found her and come to the door to inform Ian of what has befallen one of our precious pets.

The pain is almost like losing a loved one. Ian buries her under the four crowns of pampas grass that form a circle in our front garden. Pampas grass whispers constantly to itself, and we'd like to think that she is being kept company by all the sotto voce chit-chat from this seemingly sociable plant.

To distract ourselves from this sadness, I suggest that we unpack some of the boxes of books we would most like to get at, put some of the bookcases in that horrible little cubby under the south stairs, where the cubicle for the loo is, and make a sort of bookery-nook. That way, we'll be able to get at something to read, and it will, at least, look a little more pleasant under there. As it is a good-sized space, we can also put a chair in there to sit on when we're choosing what to read.

ESPECE DE VACHE!

Other distractions at that time were to come from the woman who was holding us to ransom for a ridiculously low price for our lovely house in the UK. Before we left, we had refitted the kitchen, retiled the walls and floor, and painted throughout. Since we had been there we had added a lot of hard landscaping, a large conservatory, and a swimming pool, and the fourth bedroom had been turned into a sauna room. We had also purchased a very expensive and stylish fire surround for the living room to replace the rather twee one that came with the house.

The first intimation we had of her displeasure at our immaculate residence was her resolution to get the decorators in. We were incensed! We had already redecorated, keeping it in neutral magnolia, so that she would have a clean canvas to work with – an immaculately clean one.

Her second beef was that the family bathroom, en-suite shower room, downstairs cloakroom and the kitchen all needed refitting. The house wasn't very old, and we'd already refitted the kitchen and the utility room, but there was no accounting for taste, of which she, presumably, had none.

Then she said she couldn't put up with the sauna room, and we would just have to remove the sauna before she moved in. That suited us fine, as we didn't really want to be without it, but Ian did specify that he wouldn't 'make good' when this was done. She was officially warned, and agreed with the arrangement.

The next object that fell foul of her twisted mind was the rather fabulous fireplace that we had installed, for a sum in four figures. She said it was a monstrosity that was going straight to the tip when she moved in. That was a very special purchase for us, and I asked the estate agent if we could take it when we cleared the property, as she disliked it so much and we loved it. Her answer left me speechless. We could take it, if we paid her five hundred pounds!!!

At that point, I asked the agent if he would request that old Sour Chops put the fire somewhere where it would obviously not fit, and where the sun doesn't shine, but he demurred, although sympathising with my sentiments. She was giving him a very hard time, too, and he was sick to death of her.

She had already told him that the built-in wardrobes were in a very rickety state, and some sort of adjustment to the price would have to be made. It was with a sweet smile of triumph that we informed the agent that the wardrobes she was dissatisfied with were not, in fact, built-in and would, therefore, be coming with us, so there was no cause for her to worry. Those were honest-to-goodness MFI wardrobes, built by Ian's fair hand, which had done us perfectly well over twenty years and two houses, and I might add that they're still going strong now, here in France, five years later.

TRAGEDY

We had steeled ourselves for the trip back to what was now like a former life, had arranged everything this end so that there was space where we needed things, and plenty of space to store things that would be going in rooms not yet extant.

The only fly in our ointment was on the Sunday just before we travelled. I hadn't seen Monkey since lunchtime, and neither had Ian. She was last spotted playing over at the war memorial, chasing lizards.

When I called her in the evening for food, she didn't come, and this was very unusual, as she usually came tearing through the garden at the sound of her name, and jumped up into my arms. I had a feeling of dread spread through my mind and body. She was gone. I knew she was. I couldn't feel her out there: which may seem daft, but I have never before had such a close relationship with an animal as I had with her.

The next morning she still didn't come when called, and even Ian's spirits began to sink. She might have stayed away overnight before, but she'd always been back in the morning. We kept an eye out all day, and told the neighbours. A friend of ours also relieved us of a photograph of her, enlarged it and put details of who to contact should anyone sight her, then put up copies of this all round the area. She could have wandered anywhere in the forest.

The next day we had to leave, and it was a tearful leave-taking, as I felt we should never see her again, and she'd been so special; so attuned to my thoughts, and so loving. She was a real character and all the neighbours loved her too, but would we ever see her again?

UK – PRONOUNCED YUK

All the travel arrangements had been made for us to go back to the UK to sign the final paperwork on the old house, and pack up the belongings we had left there to make the house looked loved and occupied. We'd booked the same removal company, because of their fair price and efficiency when we made our first move in January.

The first trouble we had was Ian not being able to find the front door key, as we stood in the porch of our former home at half-past midnight, and we had to rouse our erstwhile neighbours, who always went to bed early because they had young children, but they were the only other people who had a key locally. The friend who popped in every week had one, but she lived miles away, and it would have been impractical to go shooting off there at that time of the morning, when there was a perfectly good key sitting just the other side of a front door not far from ours.

We eventually managed to rouse them, apologising profusely for disturbing them at such an unsocial hour, and walked back through the front door and into the past. There were carpets here, and plugs and light sockets, and central heating, and bathrooms, and everything else we'd turned our backs on when we went running off towards the edge of the cliff, holding hands and with our eyes closed. And we'd jumped. There was no going back, now, to this soft life of comfort and warmth.

Nor did we want to. Ian had been very dissatisfied with his job since he moved to the global division of his company, and I had been bored out of my skull for the last couple of years at least, keeping a perfect home, doing my little bit of teaching, which had been considerably reduced since I'd given up teaching at college, because of the distances involved. We were alive again now, living on practically nothing and facing new challenges – such as being the *nouveaux pauvres,* instead of the *nouveaux riches* – and although there were, inevitably, hardships, we were having such great fun.

The move had made us feel young again, instead of just being the parents of four grown-up children, and grandparents to boot. We were invigorated, and had been thoroughly shaken out of our comfortable rut. What doesn't kill you makes you stronger. With the strains of the last couple of months with the house sale, we had come as close as we ever had, since meeting in 1972, to throwing in the towel, with me offering, at one point, to go back to the UK and lodge with Francis until I could find work, and earn enough to rent a place of my own.

We'd been through three recessions together, but the sheer tension and torture resulting from what was happening on the financial markets had nearly destroyed us. We had weathered the storm, however, and I felt we were a great deal stronger now than we had ever been in the past.

We had a lot of goodbyes to say in the week that we were there and, one evening, went down to the local thatched pub for a meal with our friends from the village band, of which I had been musical director. I'd had a great few years with them, and discovered talents I didn't know I possessed. It had done me the world of good, and boosted my confidence, musically, no end.

Now it was 'the end', but a riotous time was had by all, and I handed over the baton, metaphorically, to the friend who had so kindly kept an eye on the house for us, and made the effort to visit us twice and look for a new home near us. She would run things for now – until she moved to France as well, that is. She would be the third musical director they had lost to France, and I do believe that the founder members were getting a bit paranoid about the country.

We were to stay our last night with this couple, going out for another goodbye meal with them, before shipping out of the country where the rest of our families, our friends and our roots remained.

In the meantime, there was the Kynaston crew to prepare for. There were a few extra worries with our possessions this time, for we were to move the Turkish steam cabinet, the sauna, the Jacuzzi, and the almost brand new baby grand I had purchased in remembrance of my mother, who had died eighteen months before. The eighteen foot diameter by four foot deep above-ground pool we were going to leave behind, which I thought was very nice of us, as we were moving to warmer climes.

I later learnt that not only had the new owner hung NET curtains at our old dining room window, but had dismantled the pool and got rid of it. It was only two years old, built as a replacement for the slightly smaller one we had installed to see if we liked the idea. What a Grinch! And I was damned glad we were taking the sauna.

Ian dismantled it ready to be loaded, then showed me the room that he had sworn he would not make good. There was a large hole in the carpet, which was the same as laid throughout the house, even the conservatory. The walls that had held the fittings for the electric heating and lighting had wires with junction boxes sprouting from them, and the whole room looked sad, and sorry to see us go.

We were cheered immensely at that time, however, as we had a phone call from Paul to say that, after an absence of six days, Monkey had turned up safe and sound. She was filthy dirty and rather bedraggled but, apart from being very hungry, she seemed fine. Not only had he seen her, but so had some of the neighbours, and had rushed round to tell him, so that he could contact us in England.

We hardly even knew our neighbours when we lived in the UK! *Plus ça change*!

The central heating man had also been, because old Sour Chops had said the heating didn't work. We knew there was no problem with the system, because we had had it serviced just before we left in January, and no one had lived there since then. He had discovered that, as the tank was well down from the feed of oil to the boiler, the tank would have to be filled a bit, before the oil could rise sufficiently to feed the system. He kindly wrote me a letter to this effect, which we took a copy of, and left for her. No way were we going to fill her tank for her as well as selling her the house for half-a-crown!

At last we had to leave to get to our friends' house, although loading would go on during the evening. Although we would both have been happier to have seen everything stowed safely away, time had disappeared due to the late arrival of the Kynaston crew. They had been scheduled to arrive about ten, but when Ian rang them to see where they were, about midday, there were no chugging sounds of a removal van in the background, and Kynaston suddenly said, 'It's alright, boy. I can see Portsmouth now.'

'Why?' asked Ian, as we had been convinced they would be coming from Welshpool, where the depot was.

'Little spot of trouble with the ferries. Don't worry – we'll get the job done in time,' and then he was gone. Portsmouth? They weren't coming from Welshpool at all; they were coming back from the continent!

They had arrived about five o'clock, and even as we drove away, I was fretting, not so much about them finishing, but their getting something to eat before the end of the day. As it turned out, they had just wandered down to The Ship, the pub where we had eaten our final meal with the band, and when we arrived back the next morning to clean through, the only thing they had missed was a clock on the kitchen wall. They were gone, and we wouldn't see them again until sometime tomorrow.

I, however, had one last job to do, and I set to with enthusiasm. I wrote a note to our old home's new owner welcoming her to it and the area, and hoping that she'd be as happy there as we had been. I wrote it in Greek, however, and then signed it with a fountain pen in which I had red ink, and I must admit that it did make it look like the signature was in blood. This I left on the hob, then off we went to the final chapter of moving into our new way of life.

I guessed that, if she wanted it translated, she would probably have to contact The Greek Institute in London to find out who the local representative for that organisation was. It was, as it happened, ME!

COMING BACK HOME

Before I knew it, we were on the ferry the next night – the thirteenth as it happens, and I was watching the lights of Portsmouth recede into the darkness. Here I was, leaving everything I had ever known behind, and I only managed to squeeze out one measly tear.

Our week had been fraught with people, traffic, hustle and bustle. All the houses were too close together, all the roads were chock-a-block and, to quote son number two, it was 'doin' our heads in'. We were off, back to peace and quiet, and the rest of our (to me, unexpected) adventure. We'd even told people that we'd waited for the kids to grow up, so we could run away and join the circus. And they were, of course, scandalised. 'Won't you miss them?' they asked.

'Of course we will,' we replied, 'but think how much we would regret it on our deathbeds if we'd never taken this risk. It might, still, all blow up in our faces, but we'd be the poorer for not at least giving it a try.'

We arrived in France at about seven thirty the next morning, which was a Monday. We knew that lorries and trucks were not allowed to drive on Sundays, and therefore predicted that, as we had arrived early, we should reach the house by about half-past three, with the truck turning up sometime in the evening.

We had not counted on the cunning of this highly charged Welshman. He had taken a ferry that allowed him to arrive on French soil just after midnight at the very beginning of Monday, had then driven through the night, and reached our place just as we were setting off from the French ferry port.

We knew he was hyperactive, but nothing could have prepared us for the sight that met our eyes as we pulled up outside the property. The removal van was in the drive, and all our furniture was scattered on the drive and the lawn, as the extra small lorry that had been brought in, because they realised that the larger one wouldn't be enough, had had to go off to Geneva, and our piano had been one of the first things loaded on it.

That just left the big van, and I still don't understand how they could be on the road for the best part of a month, which I knew they sometimes were, and all three sleep in it for that length of time. When we offered them the use of a shower, they declined, John saying that they were saving that for a treat on the ferry back.

Not only was everything unloaded, but Kynaston had become bored, had heaved his Hungarian assistant through a windowless hole in the front of the barn, got him to unlock it from the inside, had taken out Ian's sit-on mower and mown all the lawns (two-thirds of an acre). That not being enough to keep him out of mischief, he had then armed himself with Ian's strimmer, and was half-way round the property, doing the edges, when we arrived.

After such a crowded week, we'd hoped just to get something to eat and retire early to bed, the removal van not being expected to turn up until about nine-thirty, then start unloading the next day, when we had recharged our batteries for a few hours. How naïve of us! The heaving and humping started now, and there was no way out of it. If a man who had driven through the night, then unloaded all our worldly goods, following that up with mowing our lawns and strimming our edges was up for it, who were we to say we were too tired?

It was rather unfortunate that this huge burst of hyperactive energy had resulted in the lads putting the Jacuzzi in the barn, unsupervised. Although they had put it in the correct section of the barn, it was, unfortunately, facing the wrong way, with the control panel totally unreachable at the back. True to form, however, they just told us to 'wait a mo', and shifted its enormous bulk with the minimum of fuss, considering how narrow the space in which it was to live was.

THE BABY GRAND

We really are in a very rural area and, by the time they had finished bringing in our possessions, there would have been nowhere still open to feed them, so I set to, to cook for five, and Kynaston and the two young lads with him joined us for a late supper. They weren't the same lads we had met in January, because Kynaston wore them out fast, and had to keep replacing them.

After they'd had a few beers and glasses of wine, and the head honcho had sat smoking some of the hand-rolled cigarettes, for which he used liquorice papers, he suddenly said, 'Right! What about that piano?'

'Now?' we both gasped, thinking of the alcohol that had been consumed by all three of them.

'Right now, boyo. Can you get us a couple of extra pairs of hands on this one?' It might have been late, but Ian was lucky enough to find both Paul and our French neighbour still up and willing to help, although Paul claimed a bad back and asked for light duties only.

I went and hid in the barn, my fingers in my ears, singing loudly, so that I wouldn't hear the unmusical crash as they dropped the instrument. But, my fears were unfounded, and it was safely installed with the minimum of fuss and the maximum of efficiency.

I just wish they hadn't driven into the gate-post when they left in the morning.

THE SCALES OF JUSTICE ARE REBALANCED

Two days after we arrived back, we received a frantic call from the estate agent in the UK. What had we done before we left the old house? The new owner had just moved in and called the police.

'The police?' we asked, absolutely flabbergasted. What on earth could have moved her to do that?

Now, on reflection we know he wouldn't have done it on purpose, because he was an absolutely straight and upright guy, our central-heating engineer. He'd dutifully come and done what we'd asked, so that we could leave an informed opinion of why the central heating system temporarily wasn't firing up and, as I mentioned previously, I had got a note from him, kept a copy, and left the original for the new owner.

It would seem, however, that he had been lax or distracted, and had not replaced the nut that stopped the fuel from escaping, letting it flow freely into the system. She had ordered a refill for the oil tank, then turned on the system. She had also found my welcome note (in Greek, if you remember).

When she called the estate agent, she claimed that I had left a death threat for her, the utility room and kitchen were flooded with fuel oil, and she'd informed the police of what we'd done.

He was hysterical, but we calmed him down by explaining the note – I had been teaching the language for donkey's years – and reminded him that he had the telephone number and contact address of the central heating engineer on the note he had written for the new owner. We were as innocent as new-born babes, whatever she thought. It was all just bad luck and coincidence, M'Lud. There is a God after all!

I believe in fate, and I'm sure that that Being had just stepped in on our behalf and evened the score, after all her appalling behaviour to us and her mercenary attitude to acquiring a superb property at a knock-down price. I must say, I laughed like a drain. Sometimes life just redresses the balance without one doing a thing about it.

A BIT OF A DO – FRENCH STYLE

This, our first summer, also coincided with some very important birthdays for our French neighbours opposite, Pascale and Gerard, when he would become sixty, she fifty, and we duly received an invitation to their joint celebrations. These would go on all day, and started with a walk round Lake Jemaye – for God's sake! Me, walk that far? – followed by an afternoon of organised sports – oh, no. Nobody ever picks me for their team – and an evening do in the *salle des fêtes* (village hall) – with organised games and dances. I sat quivering in a corner, snivelling like a tot that has been told to go to the naughty step, then tidy its room, in reaction to all this games-mistress boisterousness.

The first thing I did was to list my favourite sport as cards, as an attached piece of paper to return asked us to declare this. Cards had never got me into trouble – well, not much – before, and it was not too physical. I also chickened out of the walk as I was too fat, and generally too exhausted, to consider doing exercise for fun. Exercise was working, and I wouldn't have the two mixed.

I did, though, turn up in the afternoon, to find the field at the back of their house holding about a hundred relatives and friends, and all of them French. Our English neighbours Paul and Denise had been invited, but had cried off the daytime activities as they had claimed to have visitors. They were either cowards or liars. I didn't want to be here, being herded into a team that did not involve Ian, but here I was.

No, I wasn't. Here I was running as fast as a chubby body can, back home to have a good cry. I'd always hated team games at school, for the aforesaid reason that no one wanted the fat kid on their team, and I would not be treated like that lonely, sad fat kid again, at my age.

After a while Ian came over to tell me that it was all silly games, and not real, competitive ones, and that I should come back and at least watch. And I wouldn't have to go back to my team? No, I could go and sit with Paul and Denise who had also turned up and were spectating. I agreed, but if anyone even showed me a coloured band to go over my shoulder, I would be off again, trying to better the fat persons' hundred yards' dash.

The games were absolutely hilarious. Table tennis I wouldn't have minded, but this one had an unusual twist. It was to be played on a miniature table, with all team members involved, running round it in a desperate race to get to the other side before it was their turn to hit the ball.

There was a cherry stone spitting competition, at which I could hardly believe my eyes, not because of how far the stones went, but that it wasn't considered bad form to do something so yuk. It would never have happened where we used to live, but it was fun to watch. I was getting into the spirit of the occasion now.

Even more so when the next game turned out to be netball, with water filled balloons, and the hoop round Gerard's forehead, so that every time someone scored, the balloon burst all over him. So, that was why they had asked for our favourite sports, so that they could devise this crazy afternoon, at which alcohol was served at half-time.

The best race, though, was the wheelbarrow obstacle course in pairs, in which one person got into the wheelbarrow while the other pushed it round, under, over and through a series of increasingly difficult obstacles. Thrills and spills there were aplenty, as well as a great deal of honest laughter, and we went home to prepare for the evening festivities, me in a much better mood, Ian just relieved that I'd come back. As he said, I'd have kicked myself if I'd missed all that fun.

We had two hours off to prepare for the evening, and we took a bit of a rest before getting done up in our best bib and tucker. It turned out that we, Paul, Denise, and their grandson were the only English guests, but I could already feel the Gallic spirit rising in me. Perhaps it was that mid-afternoon drink, or the hideously strong concoction which had greeted every guest at the door.

Professional caterers from the school where Pascale taught had agreed to do the food. Now, don't be fooled about this school cooking stuff. This is France, after all, and the food was superb. The most I can remember about the wine was that it was plentiful.

The food was let out to us in dribs and drabs, as we had tasks to achieve first. The first one was to make up a song about the couple whose party it was to a well-known French tune, in teams again, then perform it. Sorry, guys, French not good enough for that, but Pascale didn't let that spoil her control-freakish nature. Now, we all had to learn the Macarena. And learn it we did (although I have now forgotten it) but it was surprisingly good fun.

Then there were speeches. During one of these, I slipped outside to indulge in my then (not now) beastly tobacco habit, and found myself outside with some of

Pascale's relatives. Suddenly, we were conversing, and I realised how much French I must have absorbed, sponge-like, without being aware of it. Of course, I realise that anyone from the UK who has had a couple of alcoholic beverages can suddenly become more fluent in a language they thought they had scant knowledge of, but it had never happened to me before.

Feeling rather full of myself, I went back indoors only to find Pascale asking for volunteers to do their party-piece on the stage. I immediately volunteered. You can tell by this how much I had drunk, and how flown with my own success I was. Get your head out of your arse, Madame Frazer.

As I stood up, reality sobered me slightly, and I wondered what the hell I would do. I didn't have any instruments with me, and was probably a bit (a lot) too tipsy to play any of them with any accuracy. I settled on singing, a capella, 'Plaisir d'Amour'.

Returning to my seat to a roar of applause, and with a very red face, I finally looked up to find a queue of men that stretched from my seat to the end of the hall, and beyond. 'It is traditional,' Pascale explained to me in French. 'The first lady to perform earns a kiss from all the men present.' Wow! It went on for ages, but did give me a feeling of what it must be like to be famous and horded by fans. And, I thought, I might as well enjoy it, as I'm on my last legs, looks-wise, unless some man has a fantasy about one of those very wrinkled dogs. Tonight, I was the bees' knees.

But tonight was nowhere near finished yet. There was more wine to be drunk. There were plenty more willing volunteers to go up on stage and make fools of themselves. There was more dancing to do. There were more speeches to make, more food to be eaten and the cake to be presented, not to mention coffee and liqueurs and presents.

Presents, we were present for, but, as for the rest, we

left at two o'clock, and dessert had still not been served. I think it went out at about three o'clock, and the party just carried on.

The next morning many of the party-goers had just turned into clearer-uppers, and were carrying hordes of black bags out of the hall. They had partied all night, as my mother had told me her family used to do, segueing seamlessly into Irish fried breakfasts. You might not expect potato bread and bacon here, but they had seriously celebrated all the way through the hours of darkness, and were now clearing away as if nothing unusual had happened. And, do you know, I don't think it had done. Boy, can these people, most of them older than us, party. They are THE non-stop party people.

STATUS OF UK HOUSE: What UK house?

CHAPTER EIGHT

This house eats furniture; Judith Iscariot does not live in this vicinity; Snakes; Let the refurbishment begin; *Cornichon* – or gherkins, to you; Tomatoes; A gluttony of gluts; Dwarves and henges; Not open all hours

THIS HOUSE EATS FURNITURE

Ian had suffered grave doubts about whether we would get all the older furniture we brought over the second time into the house, considering the load we had brought over in January. Oh, he of little faith! Not only did it absorb it effortlessly, but left us in no doubt that there was room for yet more, and some of the spaces would look very sparsely furnished if we didn't do something about it. After all, we were going to have a vast library upstairs to fill.

A library isn't just books. It's absolutely necessary to have lots of places to sit, with different seating for different types of reading. It's almost obligatory to have a large table, so that you can spread yourself around, so to speak.

We needed more furniture, and even my Doubting Thomas of a husband couldn't deny that. There was also an area of the barn to which there was access from the house, and we wanted to develop this as well, eventually. At the moment it housed only the Jacuzzi in one section, the other section was currently an uppy-downy bare-earthed floor. At some point, that was going to need something to go in it, although there was still so much to do that we didn't know, at that moment, what its eventual purpose would be.

We were currently locked in discussion about how to fit the new bedroom furniture in the new bedroom when it was built. Ian had the measurements and was sure it was too small. I had no such qualms but I bided my time. Once we had a floor we could walk on up there, I'd just take a piece of chalk, draw the shapes on the floor, and rest my case.

An old friend once told me that if a place you're viewing is overcrowded, and it's difficult to assess the floor space, then just look up at the ceiling. There won't be much furniture up there. Now, this is very wise advice, but, as we didn't have a ceiling upstairs, useless in this case, so I just waited patiently to be proved right. After all, we only had nine sofas and eight sideboards. A hungry library could absorb quite a lot of stuff before it was sated.

JUDITH ISCARIOT DOES NOT LIVE IN THIS VICINITY

We had a call from Kay, who swore she wanted to move as near to us as possible so that we could all four go into business together. She sounded very furtive, as she admitted that she and Robert had been to France on a house-viewing trip, and had had an offer on a property accepted.

This was great news, I thought, although I couldn't understand why she didn't tell us they were coming over, and didn't stay with us. The truth came out when I asked her where the property was, and she answered, 'Normandy.'

I have absolutely nothing more to say in this section and shall, therefore, end it here.

Actually, I will do no such thing. I just had a momentary wobble there. The friendship has survived because I realised that grudges are made of lead, and if you carry them around with you, you're the one that's going to end up dragged down and hurt. Life is too short for that sort of thing, and we're all a long time dead. An old friend takes a long time to grow, so something like that can't be discarded lightly.

We are still in touch, and I just had to swallow the fact that Kay wanted to live in the north so that it was easier for her family to visit. As I said to myself shortly after I got the news of where they were moving to, 'Get over it!'

SNAKES

This seems like a fitting next section! When we arrived here, our neighbour Paul informed us that we were in an area that had adders, and that, every spring, we should get a can of something called *Serpenticide* to spray across all accesses to the house, both doors and windows, to keep the long wiggly things out. This duly done, we then forgot about the whole serpent business, supposing it dealt with.

Not so! Ian was outside one day, when he caught one of the cats playing with something it had found that seemed to be jolly good fun. To his horror, it turned out to be not only a snake, but an adder. Without stopping to think about it, he rushed straight to his wood barn, grabbed a short-handled axe and removed its head.

A bite could have killed one of our cats. I knew a man who sang in the choir who had been bitten by one, and it was no joke. It happened during the night when he went to the bathroom. One of his cats must have brought in an adder earlier that day and broken its neck, but not killed it.

As he stood there attending to what he needed to do, the snake reared as high as it could (which was his ankle) and gave him a good chew. He ended up in hospital for a while, and said the experience was very unpleasant.

Another story came from our neighbours who one day had found that an adder had taken up residence behind their kitchen skirting-board. It stayed there for about a week, and they just left it alone, to decide for itself when to leave.

The builder, whom I had met at the choir, said that his wife had seen a pair of them in their swimming pool one day when it had been emptied, and phoned him up in absolute hysterics to get right back to the house and do something about it immediately. She wasn't to be expected to deal with such dangerous wildlife on her own.

The same builder, Beeny, when examining the roof timbers in our upstairs barn had found a long, sloughed snake skin up there, so there were plenty of the little devils about, and Ian found quite a few that season, mercilessly separating their heads from their bodies, and taking no chances, either with our health, or that of the cats. Better safe than sorry, was his opinion, and lying in a hospital bed or, even worse, being buried under the pampas grass simply wasn't an option, although I'm sure Ian wouldn't really have put me there for the sake of economy.

OUR FIRST HARVEST OH HELP!

We had never had anything significant from any garden efforts in the past but now we saw our first return. I need to make it clear that we didn't actually have to do anything to achieve this but we still felt thrilled by all the fruit on our cherry tree, which was here when we bought the property. Strolling around picking your own fresh cherries felt somehow decadent and reinforced the dream of growing and eating our own food.

However, once the initial glow had worn off, Ian realised that he had to actually pick all the cherries off the tree and he had to do it quick before the birds had them all. I remember him talking to the cats, asking them where they were when he needed them to chase the blinking birds. So began our first experience of the tyranny of the harvest.

Ian had to climb the tree to get a lot of the cherries and my heart was in my mouth watching him cling precariously to branches with one hand and picking with the other, using his makeshift cherry net made from an old onion sack secured to his belt. It didn't take long to start filling up the salad containers in two fridges and for the pressure to build to actually do something with them as you can only eat so many fresh cherries and we were not making a dent in them.

Ian had already had some discussions with friends about cherries and had found out that those with bigger trees got together to help each other pick (including using the aptly named cherry picker) all working the whole day and then they processed them together using cherry stoners, before having a well-earned meal and drink together, a jolly fun event.

We only had one small tree and had to work alone, but Ian did manage to borrow a cherry stoner which made a huge difference to the processing. It still involved us spending many hours stoning and freezing our precious harvest, but we were really living the dream and were loving it.

This was a week of frenetic activity. Ian had come to an understanding with the birds that they could have the cherries at the very top of the tree where he couldn't venture and he had finally finished clearing all the remaining branches. All the fruit was processed and we had a warm glow at our first success, bring on the next harvest!

LET THE REFURBISHMENT BEGIN

The work on the inside of the house now began in earnest, although we would have to postpone the plans for the outside. The great big old 'barn' in the other upstairs was the prime target for the first of the long list of jobs that needed to be done, and Beeny and Barney – he of the terrifying appearance – set to, to pull up all the upstairs floorboards that were rotten.

Their first discovery was that there had been a big fire down in the middle room downstairs, estimated to be about a hundred years ago. This was evidenced by the fact that all the boards they lifted were quite badly fire-damaged underneath, and this led them to a yet more sinister and dangerous discovery.

The beam that ran from the front to the back of the house was only balanced at its back end on its upright support by about three-quarters of an inch. The house is nearly three hundred years old, built without foundations on clay, so this was the product of all those years of very slight movement. We knew that the adjoining barn had been damaged by the severe drought and heatwave of 2005, and had large cracks in one section which needed to be steel-reinforced, at some point, as a result.

This, however, created a serious problem that had to be addressed immediately. If this beam lost its precarious foothold on the upright, the house might suddenly transform itself into a bungalow, and we, if at home, could find ourselves wearing the first floor as our shrouds. An Acrow prop would need to be installed without delay, and steel plates measured for and ordered.

The visible bit of the beam in the middle room was boarded round, with large bolts going through the structure at one end, so Beeny stripped off the cladding at the back end of it, only to have a historical rats' nest cascade down on his head, in a shower of rags and other detritus; fortunately no historical rats appeared to have been at home at the time. He estimated it to be about a century old.

The lifting of the upstairs floorboards, which covered two-thirds of the house, also brought to light other problems. Although the two main rooms below this area had ceilings downstairs, the hall and the loo/bookery-nook did not. This meant that a 'modesty' lid needed to be placed over the ghastly little loo cubicle, so that one didn't have an audience every time one went there to conduct business, and it has to be borne in mind that this was the only lavatory in the property. It's very disconcerting to be having a quiet 'clock' with a book and look up to see a face staring down at you, accompanied by a cheery wave.

The other problem was that the floorboards had been fixed so securely and had been in place for such a long time that, when the boards above the door from the middle room into the hall were wrenched out of their ancient resting place, a crack appeared from the ceiling to the top of the door, the lintel (stone) cracked, and the whole doorframe dropped marginally.

This only became apparent when I complained that the door was suddenly difficult to open and I couldn't understand why. Barney understood only too well, and another Acrow prop appeared in our lives. We now had two in the same room and, at first, it was very disconcerting.

An examination of the roof timbers also revealed an area that would have to have steel work fitted, and we were already aware of the steel work that would have to be done in the barn to stop the back wall falling off. Fortunately, we had never believed that the project would just sail through smoothly, understanding that, with a very old property, some of the problems will be hidden. These could have proved serious to the structure of the building without prompt attention, and we had a contingency fund to deal with just such a situation.

On receiving the original estimates for the work, split into labour and materials, we knew the materials budget wouldn't be too far off kilter, but we mentally doubled the labour budget, as a way of coping with extra work, and also mentally put aside a contingency for emergencies.

I ran the project budget, keeping a record of every

receipt, including those piddling little ones for just a few screws or nails, tallied these each Friday, subtracted them from the total budget for the job in hand, then we tallied up the wages and handed them out, this being subtracted from the labour on the appropriate page of my records.

A little ruse I also employed was to have a page for 'miscellaneous' expenses, for I knew there were things that Ian wanted and which the new rooms upstairs would need, but which were not covered by the refurbishment fund, which had just been divided into labour and materials. I had visions of running out of money on the project, then Ian saying, 'But we never got our American fridge/freezer. And we haven't got any bookcases or furniture for the library. It's just a huge empty room with boxes of books in it.'

Of course, I never really explained this extra page to him, as he rarely looked at the records I was keeping, but as things were reduced for sale that I knew we would need, I'd persuade him to buy them, and when he asked how we were going to justify the expense, I just pointed out to him that, as they were in the finished master-plan, they would have to be sorted out some time, as we didn't want to do without when it was all over. Everything was in hand. He trusted me, thank God!

Things had to be thus, for the budget for the work that we had originally hoped for was now halved by the disastrous sale price of our UK house, and we had a lot less to work with. Some things had to be bought, whether we liked it or not, as they couldn't wait.

All our white goods in the old house were built in and, although we had had to buy some replacements when we first arrived, the fridge in our kitchen was over twenty years old and on its last legs. The American jobbie might sound a bit over the top, but it wasn't. We've always been used to lots of chilling space, and our freezer was now out in the barn, not a pleasant trip across the courtyard when it was raining, blowing a gale or freezing. Chilled water and ready-made ice were all Ian really wanted as a luxury, and I was determined that he should have them. Dammit, he'd worked long and hard enough to have a little of what he craved, in his new life.

CORNICHON – OR, GHERKINS TO YOU!

The fruits of Ian's labours in the garden had started with a trickle. Now the trickle was increasing to a flood, and it was time to work out what we would do with our garden's bounty. Blanching and freezing was an obvious option for the surplus we couldn't eat now, as it would see us through the unproductive months, when we had little on offer. Jams and chutneys were also an excellent idea, as they would give us a taste of summer in the winter months, and remind us why we (Ian) did it in the first place.

It was also a revelation to be able to grow vegetables that had been impossible to rear in the UK which, inevitably, meant that we had no idea how long it took for plants to produce ripe specimens. There are only so many seed packets you can read, when they're all in a language which you are still in the early stages of wrestling with.

He had planted a long bed of gherkins along the fence to the west of the property, and strong healthy plants grew there now. Ian had some idea that they'd be like courgettes. Their fruits developing after the flower had died away, in the same place. Not so! During this month the temperature soared to nearly forty degrees, and Ian was run ragged watering the vegetable garden.

One evening he noticed that the gherkin plants had suffered rather from the sun, and that their leaves had a rather droopy appearance. Approaching for a closer look, now able to see below the leaves, he looked down and started with horror. Without a word to me, he collected a large green trug from the barn and filled it with as many of the gherkins that he could cram in, then trotted into the house with a puzzled expression on his face.

The first I knew of it was when I heard him come through the front door calling out, 'Anyone for gherkins?' He appeared in the kitchen, his trug full to the handle with the fruits of the sweat of his brow, all of them the size of a child's forearm.

'What the hell are they?' I asked, visions of triffids dancing in my head, but no idea how he could have got hold of such alien seed.

'They're gherkins!' he stated baldly.

'They can't be!' I retorted. 'You'd never have let them grow that big. You're pulling my leg, aren't you? Gherkins are the size of my thumb, and you get loads of them in a jar.'

'Nope!' he replied, now allowing a smile to break out on his face at the absurdity of it all. 'They really are gherkins. Apparently they grow *under* the leaves. I didn't think we'd managed to grow anything at all, then I saw this lot. Pickled or frozen?' he asked, assuming an absolutely straight face.

'Is that all of them?'

'Nope!'

When we finally weighed the crop, we had forty-two pounds of gherkins, and very little idea of what to do with such monsters.

We eventually peeled some of them, cut them and pickled them. Others we froze, as we had been told that the French make a delicious soup with them. That solved the problem about what to do with the rest of them. We distributed them to anyone we knew, who accepted them with grateful thanks and, not only relieved us of our weighty problem, but earned us a house-point locally, as well.

TOMATOES

You've guessed it. Over-production strikes again! Ian had enthusiastically planted one hundred and twelve tomato seedlings which I'd raised for him, a hundred and eleven of which 'took'. There were a great many varieties in that planting, and we looked forward to plum tomatoes for cooking, giant tomatoes that would give us sandwich-sized slices, little cherry tomatoes that would roast in olive oil and garlic like a dream, and tiny little cocktail ones that could be popped into the mouth, to be enjoyed with a glass of wine.

He was also growing miniature fruits that were shaped like pears, and yellow in colour, and which proved irresistible for casual nibbling, and some of the green zebra variety that were almost too beautiful to eat. So many varieties and colours made for an eye-dazzling tomato salad, and the abundance with which they ripened meant that we should be able to make a large amount of chutneys, sauces, soups and passata – again for a flavour of summer in the winter.

With so many plants though, I used to dread him coming in from watering. Most nights he'd come in with a full trug of tomatoes which, when weighed, would prove to come to over a stone. Thank goodness we had enough fridge room to keep them until we had time to turn them into something else.

Some evenings he'd have me fooled, bring in the usual full trug, wait for me to weigh them, then start emptying his shorts' pockets of all the cherry tomatoes he didn't have room for in the trug. That was always a match to my blue touch paper, and I sometimes didn't see the funny side of so much of the same.

We started not only to make little gifts of them to our friends, but to swap them for things we didn't have or hadn't grown. A couple we knew in the commune kept chickens, of which we had none yet, so we swapped excess freshly-grown vegetables and fruit with them, for free-range freshly-laid eggs.

This only took us a small way towards using our glut, and it wasn't long before our friends turned up their noses at our tomatoes, as they were drowning in their own. Time to get creative.

We started first with chutneys. Picking some of the glut while still green helped us here. It meant that not only would we not have such an enormous amount of vegetable matter to process in the near future, but that we could have green tomato chutney now, which was one of our favourites from the very early days of our marriage.

We could also use the red tomatoes, not only in red tomato chutney, but in other yummy bottled condiments. Operation Chutney commenced, some of the enormous preserving pans we were using taking up to eight hours to reach the right consistency on our useless modern cooker. Sore feet and aching legs were about to become a part of everyday life.

When we had made all the chutney we could cope with and more, we started on soups and sauces for the freezer. After that came passata for jarring, for use in making sauces on the hoof. The rest we froze, so that they could be tossed into stews, casseroles and roasting pans, until the next season started. I have never seen so many tomatoes together before, in one freezer. Heaven help us when we started freezing other produce. At this rate we'd need another freezer just to cope.

In the end I started dreaming about tomatoes, and was really ready for a change, when Ian began persecuting me with gluts of other vegetables.

A GLUTTONY OF GLUTS

I realise that I have probably not used the correct collective noun for the title of this section, but in retrospect, it seems to sound perfect, reflecting the feeling of being overwhelmed, during that first summer of harvest.

From green to red, we now had a colour change to yellow, as the sunburst squashes started to ripen in abundance. It was a vegetable that I hadn't used before, so I sincerely hoped we'd like it, as I threw it in to roast with some other suitable vegetables.

Delicious! was our immediate decision, although I was slightly disconcerted to find that it made a slight squeaking noise against the teeth as I bit into the chunks. It was a firm hit, though, and I even invented a recipe with this yellow disc as its main ingredient, so that we could consume as many as possible, rather than freezing them, which would somewhat alter the texture. We couldn't cope, though, and bags of them went into the freezer against lean veg times. I was sure we could live with the result because of the lovely taste, and roasting should disguise the fact that they had been in the freezer.

Another change of colour, and courgettes hit the chopping board, and we ate them stuffed, stewed and roasted, with the inevitable overspill for less bounteous, colder times. Butternut squashes soon started propelling themselves into the kitchen. These, however, on advice from a gardening book, suggested that they needed to be hardened off before consumption, so they had to spend ten days in the sun after harvesting, before being stored in the barn, to be used as needed.

Cucumbers we found we could grow profusely on the compost heaps and our salads were a delight, when added to home-grown radishes, tomatoes, onions, lettuce, small perpetual spinach leaves, rocket, grated carrot, beetroot ... The list of ingredients seemed endless.

Our store cupboard and freezers were now looking mightily full, and we still hadn't dealt with the pumpkins which, although they would not be harvested for some time, were lurking all over the garden in ever-increasing numbers, and beginning to look like they would be a bit of a handful (never mind a mouthful) when they were ready to be cut free from their moorings in the ground.

The garlic, which had been one of the first things planted, grew well, and after harvesting it the two of us sat contentedly in the barn at a plastic garden table, plaiting it into bundles. One of these Ian took over to our French neighbours opposite because, even though their property was only yards away from ours, they had never been able to grow this fragrant and delicious bulb. What a coup, eh? Gifting garlic, grown by the English, to the native French.

DWARVES AND HENGES

Some of the other first vegetables that Ian had put in the ground were green and yellow French beans, peas and broad beans. We had bought the seeds for these from a local gardening-cum-do-it-yourself shop, and had managed to understand every word printed on the packet except for one, and this was the word *nain*.

We didn't see what difference one word could make to the general growing of these plants, and just got on with sowing them. Ian then built a rather fearsome structure out of wood which we named 'Pea-Henge', and strung it with wires ready for the climbers to do their stuff and reach for the sky.

Which they didn't! I finally looked up *nain* in the French dictionary, only to discover that it meant 'dwarf'. Pea-Henge had been an effort in vain, as these things would never get above knee height, and to make things worse, he had put in the cross bars just below the height of the top of my head, so that whenever I was harvesting any of the things, I usually got a wallop round the head to help me on my way.

I'd never tried the yellow variety of French beans before, and they proved to be a delight on the taste-buds and a bright visual treat on the plate. These would be our beans of choice for the future.

The broad beans, as required by tradition, began to suffer from black fly, and abundant washing-up liquid in water was thrown over them to discourage the dirty little beasts. The pods were such a disappointment to empty, though, as they were so sticky and furry, the beans on the inside so small, that we decided they were not worth the effort. Although I was to miss them keenly in the future, and request that we grow some more, and said I'd do all the pod-lobbing.

NOT OPEN ALL HOURS

Having been brought up in a churchy sort of way, with Sunday school and all that jazz, I remember being scandalised when the subject of opening shops on the Sabbath was first mooted. But, you know how things are? You get swept along with the tide, and find that going out for pleasure shopping on a Sunday is a regular occurrence. Crikey! When I was little there weren't even any newspapers on Good Friday, let alone anyone having the brass-necked cheek to open a shop.

No such problem here, though. Good Friday is not recognised as a bank holiday, and was just another working day. On Sundays, though, the only shops open, and then for only a couple of hours in the morning, were newspaper shops so that the men could get their paper and baccy; florists, so that flowers could be bought for relatives to be visited later in the day; and patisseries, so that cakes could accompany said flowers. The other shops did not open.

Much to our extreme annoyance, neither did they open between the hours of noon and 2 p.m. on other days. Apart from the odd supermarket, everything else was shut up tight as a drum, and all paid-for parking was free so that the French tradition of a two-hour break for lunch *à la famille* could be observed. The most annoying thing was that this was when we took a break, and all the DIY shops were also locked up like Fort Knox, as they were on the Sabbath. How the French ever shop for DIY materials and gardening stuff I have not yet worked out.

Back to the weekends, though. We had not realised what a nation of ferocious hunters this is, and put that with the fact that we lived in the Double Forest, and you have a very interesting situation on Sundays. Each week men in yellow jackets, with white vans and slavering dogs, lined the roads at the edge of the areas of forest, positively bristling with guns.

For a while, at least, we tried to keep our cats in on that day, for the shots went off incessantly, and it was not unheard of for an over-zealous hunter to pursue a cat into its own back garden and shoot it before the very eyes of its horrified owner. We referred to the straggling lines of armed men as the good old boys, but they sure did love their guns and their dogs, these latter being untrainable as house dogs, and always kept outside.

One calamitous combination of adrenaline-drenched man and over-excited young dog occurred in the next village, when the man had left the safety catch off his gun, the young dog jumped up, and gun went off, and took his hand with it. It is a common weekend hazard here and, although we cannot keep our cats caged up indoors as we did in the early days, we still sometimes worry about them when we hear shooting.

An added 'bonus' to this Sunday cacophony is when the nearest vineyard owner sets up a bird-scarer in his vineyard, so the almost indistinguishable shots of this also punctuate the lazy hot days for us. It certainly dissuades you from taking a nap in the garden and keeps you working.

Life here has a very different rhythm. We got used to it

without realising it and, only on a brief visit back to the UK, did we realise how much we had adapted. I missed the babble of French voices and the road signs. I almost missed the midday closing hours. I certainly missed the uncrowded shops and the slower tenor of life. Slowly but surely, we were becoming more French.

One type of establishment that didn't close at lunchtime, and certainly not on a Sunday, was the restaurant/bistro and, although we were poor as church mice, we did make a couple of visits to inexpensive examples.

One such visit was to a nearby village where the old post office had been turned into a restaurant, Sunday lunch being at an all-in price, including wine. We went with some neighbours who had highly recommended it, and our hopes were raised; but then, we had been brought up on English Sunday roasts.

The soup course consisted of the water – with additional whole cabbage leaves – of the water in which the *pot au feu* (boiled meat and vegetables) had been cooked, with lots of bread so crusty I'm surprised they didn't have a dentist on hand for running repairs.

The main course was the aforementioned boiled meat, surrounded by the vegetables that had been boiled with it, and some more tooth-cracking bread, dessert being ice-cream from a well-known manufacturer, still in its individual plastic container. The main attraction seemed to be that when the litre carafe of wine was empty, another was brought to the table; no extra charge.

Cheese and biscuits served, as always, before dessert, was a little bit of plastic-packed rubber cheese and a pair of individually cellophane-wrapped crackers. Yes, it was cheap, but then it needed to be. There was little of nutritional value in it, and certainly nothing of gourmet merit.

Our friends just got on with the wine though, happily

chattering away, whereafter we were motioned to repair to the bar with them, where more alcohol was flowing. What a pity we had come in their car. The drive home was one of the most terrifying journeys I have ever endured, and this was an experience we have never repeated, not least because the food is so much better at home.

As I have emphasized, this was not a time of eating out much, even in frugal style, and it was quite a bit later before we ventured out again, this time with a couple of visitors. The restaurant's name, in English, was The Open Bottle. This should have warned us.

The owners had advertised on the local internet site for a special Friday night menu, and we were seduced. Following the directions to the letter, we came to the road, just off which it was supposed to be situated, but there was only one establishment with tables and chairs outside, and there was a mere glow from inside; no real light showing at all. Surely it couldn't have closed down between us booking a table and arriving?

Full of trepidation, we approached in the car, to see that it was merely shuttered against the outside world, and went in to find that we were the only customers. There was an old man behind the bar who said he ran the place with his wife. Where were the locals having an early evening drink, we wondered, this being a Friday night, but did not dare ask.

The tables and chairs in the bar area looked like they had been accumulated from a number of closing-down restaurants over quite a few years, and the thought of sitting eating in that dreary, poky hole was not very appealing. As soon as we declared ourselves as M et Mme Frazer, the old guy shuffled from behind the bar and flung open a door in the back wall, behind which lay a huge dining room, laid out for dozens of covers.

We were to be the first people into it tonight – and might I add, the only inhabitants of it. We went to the bar for an *apero* and the man's wife came out to take our orders. She was just tottering away when the realisation that both of them were absolutely rat-arsed dawned on us. No wonder they had no customers.

But we were English, and we could not cut and run in the face of fire, so we doggedly pursued the meal to the bitter end, the woman so drunk that, instead of clearing plates, she merely swept them aside and sat down with us to tell us all about their family.

Ian finally cleared away and handed her the detritus with a fierce glare. Before we could get out, even when the meal was over, we had to go to look at a display of one of their young relatives playing football and posing with the team, accompanied with a life history. It was so grim that I can confirm that we high-tailed it without even finishing one bottle of wine between the four of us, and vowed never to eat there again.

Someone had definitely opened the bottle too early in that establishment. When we told this story to a friend, he said he had made the same mistake, with identical results, and made the same vow never to cross the threshold again.

CHAPTER NINE

The joys of jamming; The joys of musical jamming; Downhill all the way; The joys of wine and its role in making new friends

THE JOYS OF JAMMING

Title of this section aside, one of the joys of this time of the year was definitely flinging open the bedroom windows in the morning, hanging out the duvet to air, and looking out over the fields and trees to the wooded hills beyond. The view was east, and the spectacle absolutely beautiful. The same could be said for the sunset view from the back of the barn, which looked south-west. We really had landed in a little bit of paradise here, and it lifted our hearts, especially on a sunny day.

Soft fruits became the next priority. The seasons aren't quite the same here. The soft fruits seem to go on forever, and the apples ripen early. In our garden we had raspberries, strawberries, figs, gooseberries, blackberries and a selection of currants. We also had plums, cherries, peaches, apricots, nectarines, pears and apples from our trees. All of these fruits I shall deal with in one fell swoop here, rather than split them up into a series of slightly disjointed activities.

I know that most people know how to make jam, and a great number of them do so, so I shall merely indicate which jams we found the most mouth-watering and delicious from the many we made. We also found our glut of preserved goods a great product range the following year when our *bourg* had a *vide grenier* – a boot sale –

where they proved an undoubted hit on our stall, and bulked up our earnings nicely on what we had grown from seed.

Fig jam, when enlivened with strawberries is unbelievably delicious. Home-made plum jam, the same, as is home-made apricot. Cherries are best left for freezing or for pies in this household, as Ian never managed to get his cherry jam to set satisfactorily, and ended up with several jars of preserved cherries in a sticky sauce. It was good for pouring over ice-cream, and the cherries were useful in cake-baking, so maybe, on reflection, we had discovered something really useful by accident. We're still thinking about that one.

The best of the lot, though, was the blackcurrant jam. Small in quantity because we didn't have a lot of bushes, it was really ambrosial. Ian also made some blackcurrant ice-cream which was delightfully sharp and tangy; the most unusual ice-cream I have ever tasted, and the first mouthful really surprised some of our guests at supper one evening, when it was served for dessert.

THE JOYS OF MUSICAL JAMMING

Easter would see my first performance with the choir. I had joined at a point when the group was about eighteen months old, and was trying out its first serious work. Before, they had presented variety-style shows with songs from the shows and other well-known numbers. This concert was to be in the *Collégiale* church in the nearest town, and we would be accompanied and complemented by an orchestra that a double-bass player who had been singing with us had organised.

They were mostly English musicians, and the conductor would be flying over from the UK too. We should also have the benefit of professional soloists, and it was to be something of a red-letter day if we pulled it off, because there were no other choirs in the area that put on a performance in this manner.

Of course, there was great excitement as well as trepidation, but my only worry was that I'd had 'one of my chests' and was also feeling very worn out and ragged, finding everyday tasks almost impossible to perform. I ignored the way I was feeling as much as possible, for not only was there the concert to look forward to, but we were expecting Stephanie, her husband and two sons in the near future, and I didn't want to be ill for her first visit here.

The last time we'd seen them had been June, but then only for an hour, before our ferry took us off in pursuit of the furniture lorry and its insane owner. We saw her second son for the first time then, for he hadn't been born until the end of April, and their visit was anticipated with joy.

The day of the concert dawned hot and sunny, and was to prove the warmest of the year. Inside the church, as we rehearsed in the afternoon, it was blessedly cool, but outside the sun beat down ferociously. We were to rehearse all afternoon, then take a two-hour break before re-gathering again for the real thing.

The church, being ancient, had no parking of any kind and was situated on a steep hill, which made it very difficult for me, suffering as I was at the time from chronic asthma, to walk any distance. As we approached the church for the second time that day, this time for Ian to remain for the performance, instead of just dropping me off, one of the French tenors indicated an entrance into a garden that looked private to me, but he explained that he knew the people who owned it, and it would be acceptable for us to park there, given my condition. What a kind man!

The performance was warmly greeted and went off as best as it could have, given our inexperience. It was certainly a one-off in this area, and I learnt a thing or two about French protocol from it, too. I found out that, even though it was high summer and almost unspeakably hot, all women had to wear long-sleeved garments, as no one (or, at least, no woman) was allowed to appear with bare arms within the church.

I also learnt that what is an insult after a performance in England is the highest accolade here, just across the Channel. At the end of the evening, after a considerable amount of applause and whistling, a slow hand-clap started somewhere in the church, and was soon taken up by every member of the audience.

Surely we hadn't done that badly, I thought, then someone hissed in my ear that this was the equivalent of *encore*. The French don't actually use the word '*encore*'. They'd loved what we'd done and wanted more. In the future, I was to see an English conductor leave his podium and then the performance area because he thought he was being criticised, when exactly the opposite was true. So close in proximity are the two countries but so different are their ways.

I went home that night on a high, not having been involved in choral singing in this form for years. Yes, I'd sung in choirs all my life, but most of them were of the school or church variety. It was a very long time since I had sung with a large choral group, and it was exhilarating in the extreme. Suddenly, I couldn't wait to find out what we were going to sing next.

DOWNHILL ALL THE WAY

The beginning of the month was okay, with various visits to Gerard and Pascale and Paul and Denise for *apéros* or supper, with the reciprocation of these visits giving us other views on how we were doing with the house. Pascale seemed to think that I had a decent eye for interior design, but would not be able to see the finished product until we had had the new upstairs built; the old wormy, burnt floorboards now a thing of the past. What we had done, though, she liked, *plus ça change*-ing all over the ground floor, while we thought: you ain't seen nothing yet, Madam.

About the middle of the month, however, I began to feel listless, tired all the time, and began to swell up as if I were eating for five. My limbs were too heavy to move, and I was very emotional.

The rest of the month of August passed in a blur for me. I was feeling more and more exhausted, if such a thing was possible, and began to think that there was something seriously wrong with me. I went to the doctor of course, but after asking me if I was diabetic, to which I answered 'no', she didn't do any tests, but requested that I make an appointment with a neurosurgeon, as my toes had started to go numb, and my feet and legs were very painful, making it hard for me to stand for any length of time, or to walk more than a few yards.

It almost seemed like making the jams and chutneys had broken me, and even lifting my arms to get dressed in the morning was becoming a problem. My brain seemed to be slowing up too, and I was finding it more and more difficult to hold an intelligent conversation. ('No change there, then!' says Ian.) I found, also, that my varifocal glasses were becoming less effective than before. This I put down to not having seen an optician for two years, but that was just a straw to grasp, while the rest of me was drowning.

In the choir's summer break, my world shrank to the four walls of our home, going up to bed becoming a climb akin to that of Everest, so weak and exhausted was I feeling. I can write little of this period, as I don't remember much about it. I spent a lot of time sleeping, then waking up just to feel as if I hadn't rested at all. It would all have to come to a head soon, but, being an intransigent person, that was not to be for a few weeks yet.

THE JOYS OF WINE AND ITS ROLE IN MAKING NEW FRIENDS

One evening I do remember with unexpected clarity during this period, is one spent in a neighbour's garden sipping *apéros* and nibbling nuts, olives, and delicious little slices of charcuterie and sausage. We had been introduced to many new people, as well as remaking the acquaintance of some we had met but not seen much of.

One couple arrived very late; in fact, just in time for the first drops of a shower to fall, and for all of us to move indoors. We sat together with the newcomers, and I noticed how quickly the lady swigged wine. Well, in for a centime, in for a euro. I matched her, glass for glass, and so did Ian and her husband. Eventually it was time to go, and we asked them if they would like a look inside our house, which they eagerly if a little incoherently agreed to, and the four of us began a somewhat zig-zagging walk across the road.

Once inside, we gave them the once over, which included a torch to see up the southerly downstairs, as there was no electricity upstairs there. Then Ian opened some more wine. How on earth do occasions like this happen? Not only did we get gloriously drunk, but became firm friends in this alcoholic bonding process.

Although they shall remain nameless to protect the guilty, the chap drove them home, and we have met on a regular basis ever since, though now without alcohol as all of us have more or less given up on it. We play killer cards and vie over who has made the most weird or wonderful buy at a *brocante* or flea market. We get by!

CHAPTER TEN

Friday is bankruptcy day; A lovely visit from family; The dark shadow of illness; An encounter with a really low blood sugar level; The first attempt on my life in a French hospital, Front door blues

FRIDAY IS BANKRUPTCY DAY

Shortly after work had begun on ripping up the floorboards in the first floor 'barn', Barney went back to the UK for his annual trip as a volunteer helper at a disabled summer camp, something he has done for years. This was not just for personal satisfaction, but because it reminded him how lucky he was to be whole and leading a normal life. He's quite a guy under that gruff exterior.

During this time Beeny called in the services of a labourer, as the job was one that needed two people, and we went along with this quite happily while Barney was away. When he returned, however, the labourer stayed on ... and on ... and on.

Things came to a head when Ian noticed that this third member of the team actually had little to do, and was really just marking time every day. When he conveyed this information to me, the monster in me made an appearance. Her name is Mrs Black, and she takes over when I'm being too soft on life in general.

'Do you know how much money we're paying out every Friday?' I asked Ian and he totted it up, only to look absolutely staggered at the sum that having three men working on the property totalled. 'This cannot go on!' Mrs

Black was on a roll now. 'If we carry on like this we're going to be out of money in no time and the job nowhere near finished, even with our slashed-back requirements. Something has to be done!'

A quick glance at how much work was left to do, how much money there was in the pot, and the Friday wages bill made it obvious that something had to go, and what had to go was the labourer. Having made the decision, I locked Mrs Black back in her box and suggested that Ian was the man of the house, so he should be the one to do the firing, then I went and hid somewhere, while the news was imparted.

What we were trying to achieve was, in effect, building a brand new apartment in the hundred square metres of the large upstairs, and the skilled building work needed to be done by professionals. It was OK for us to do the unskilled jobs like painting and decorating, but neither of us knew anything about laying wooden floors, or building walls to split up the space into the master bedroom and en-suite, and a library, which would eventually occupy the area up there.

It followed, then, that we had to preserve enough funds for two people to do this, and not pay three and leave ourselves short when it came to luxuries like ceilings and doors and all that sort of fiddle-faddle. If we wanted to survive financially, we had to be hard-nosed about it. The labourer left on Friday with his last fistful of our euro-bucks.

A LOVELY VISIT FROM FAMILY

My health continued to deteriorate, and I went to the doctor once more, just before Stephanie and Co. arrived. I really was in a parlous state by then, but the doctor's words did not suit my plans at all. She insisted that I went straight to hospital that same day but I explained that I couldn't do that, or I wouldn't see my grandchildren, and I hadn't seen one of them for some time, and the other, only for an hour since he had been born.

You know what doctors are like! She was horrified. How could I be so lax as to neglect my health? she wanted to know. There was no way I was going to change my mind, so we compromised. She would give me a letter for the hospital and, as soon as Stephanie and Co. departed these shores, I would make an appearance in A&E with my letter.

I struggled on, hardly able to walk now, and needing help with dressing, but you know how stubborn a mother and grandmother can be when it comes to the possibility of not seeing her sorely missed chickens and grand-chickens. There was no way I was going to be found languishing in a hospital bed while my family was over. On this point, I was adamant, as they were only coming for five days.

We knew our first grandson James, because we had had time to get to know him over a few years before we left, but Jack had been born after we left the UK, and I wanted to make the first steps in building a relationship with this youngest member of our family.

Ian picked them up from the airport, leaving me behind, not just because of how weak and incapacitated I was, but because there simply wasn't room in the car for more than three adults and two children, who both needed a child seat of some sort.

I was, in fact, glad to be left behind, so exhausted had I become, and I relished the thought of a few hours of silence, so that I could just curl up on the sofa and sleep. I could hardly keep my eyes open, and welcomed the opportunity to have a little daytime zizz without being told to wake up or I'd never sleep that night. Oh yes I would!

It was a joy to see them again, and to get a proper look at little Jack, although he grizzled the whole time he was here; something unheard of in his own home but, as I explained at the time, he was in a strange house with people he didn't know, so that wasn't at all surprising – just a little irritating.

It was Stephanie's birthday just after she arrived, and we had a lovely family meal in celebration, and then things took a turn for the worse. The next day Ian decided he'd mow the grass (he's better at escape than the residents of Colditz Castle), but decided that he'd take James for a ride on his mower. Obviously James was really excited, and happy family holiday snaps were taken of him sitting just in front of his granddad, driving round the garden on the big red *tracteur*.

They had almost finished the front lawn when Ian's attention was drawn to something lying half-in and half-out of his wood barn, so he stopped, dismounted and went to investigate. What he found was his beloved cat, Marbles, stone dead and as stiff as a board. There was not a mark on him. He was just dead.

Now, this cat had followed Ian around like a dog, and had a huge personality – Ian even bought him his own brand of cheesy cocktail biscuits, which he fed him a few of every night at *apéro* time. Whenever Ian sat down, or sprawled on the sofa, Marbles was there on his lap or his chest, purring like a noisy engine. When he was in the garden working, Marbles would follow his every step, occasionally trying to scale his jeans to get a cuddle, and he was a big, big cat. And now he was gone.

It felt as if a big, black cloud had suddenly eclipsed the sunlight, and we were all plunged into a deep gloom. I crouched down, nursing the lifeless form in my arms and kissing its head, while Ian dug another grave in the centre of the four crowns of pampas grass. He had not had so close a relationship with a cat since his Blue Burmese, Kelly Finn, was hit by a car and killed in the late seventies. He was devastated.

Even now he cannot talk about this day, and, five years

later, only last week, was he able to purchase a pack of those particular cheesy snacks again. Although he and Marbles both used to love them, he hasn't been able to face having them in the house again, until now.

THE DARK SHADOW OF ILLNESS

When our visitors had left, Beeny's wife volunteered to come to the hospital with us to present the letter from the doctor, as our French was much too fragmentary to deal with medical-speak, and we duly presented ourselves in A&E at the hospital in Périgueux. We arrived, unfortunately, just as the French, by tradition, have lunch, and had a wait of over two hours before anyone was full enough to see us.

When I was seen, however, everything happened with great speed. Mrs Beeny accompanied me to the cubicle where I lay on a trolley, while temperature and blood pressure were checked. She stood by staunchly when my reflexes were checked, as the numbness was now spreading to my legs, which were swollen like balloons. My left leg was in such a bad way that I had no reflex at all, and couldn't even feel the hammer on my knee.

She was very calm until blood had to be taken. The dear lady has a horror of needles, and began to yelp and cringe, as if the needle were looking for a vein in *her* arm. I just lay there, certain I had something terminal, and just waiting for the diagnosis to be over so I could find out how long I had left to live my new life.

Within a few minutes a word I didn't understand started to be bandied around, which sounded like 'jabbet'. I had no idea what it meant, but it seemed that that was what was wrong with me, so I just waited until someone could inform me of what it meant. It didn't take long before one of the doctors pulled the English word out of his limited vocabulary and told me I had diabetes. Ian and I so like to do things together, and he had been diagnosed two or three years earlier with the same condition.

Mrs Beeny was allowed into the cubicle again, but the next part of the procedure was to get a cannula into my left arm, so that they could put me on an insulin pump, before being formally admitted to the diabetes ward. Did that woman scream? She had to be asked to leave again, while one of the doctors berated her for her fuss, as it wasn't her arm that was being cruelly stabbed in an effort to locate a vein. (My veins are deep in the flesh, and so shy they tend to hide at the first hint of unwanted attention.)

When Ian had been diagnosed, his reading on the English scale of measuring blood sugar (normally less than 7) had been 28. Although I said we like to do things together, I was flabbergasted when they translated my French reading (different scale) into the English one, and came up with 28! Talk about Darby and Joan!

AN ENCOUNTER WITH A REALLY LOW BLOOD SUGAR LEVEL

We had our blood sugar levels tested six times a day in the hospital, from waking to turning in for the night, and when I was first admitted, the treatment I would eventually be placed on was unknown, the only way to find the right one being by trial and error.

Some of the drugs used did not seem to bring down the level very much, even with a compliant diet, but they couldn't start those until I'd been on an insulin pump for several days, to stabilise me.

I cannot remember the name of the one that had a really dramatic result, but I do recall sitting on my bed quite late in the evening, chatting to the Englishwoman in the other bed, with whom I was sharing a room. As we talked, I began to feel rather distant and fuzzy. I told her I was feeling rather off, but she dismissed it, saying that it was probably just the new medication.

Boy! Was she right! Before long I had broken out into a cold sweat and begun to shake like an aspen leaf. I called as best as I could for her to ring for help, because by now I was beginning to lose consciousness. She thought I was mucking about at first, but when she came over to my bed, she realised I was deadly serious, and rang for a nurse.

My level, when checked, proved to be desperately low. On the French scale it would have been good to be anywhere between eighty and a hundred and twenty. Mine was fifty-seven and dropping. The kind nurse immediately administered a glass of fruit juice, which is high in sugar and very fast-acting.

My state of consciousness wasn't falling for that one. It allowed me to come back halfway, but wouldn't comply fully until I'd been fed several biscuits as well.

What was very interesting about identifying this feeling was that, although it had been extreme in this case, it was something I'd been suffering from, to a lesser degree, in the UK for years. It happened virtually every day, between half-past four and half-past five, when I was teaching at home. I'd have to rush off to the kitchen, and neck several Rich Tea biscuits and a large glass of water, before I could carry on with the lessons.

I'd been tested several times for diabetes over the years, because I also suffered from chronic abscesses, which can indicate a high blood sugar level. Only ten days before I was admitted to the hospital, Ian had used his testing kit and done a blood test for me, and my level was normal. How bizarre is that?

THE FIRST ATTEMPT ON MY LIFE IN A FRENCH HOSPITAL

Being admitted to hospital threw up a whole new set of problems with language and communication, one of which could have cost me my life, had I not been paying attention to detail.

I was put in a room (all either single or double – no large wards here, my dears) – with another English patient who had been here longer than me, but spoke even less French, not even understanding *bonne nuit* when a nurse wished her goodnight. I was quite happy about this, and we soon got to know each other.

One of the first things the staff did was to put us on a twenty-four hour fluid test. This meant that we had to collect all our wee for that period of time, and pour it into a very large glass container – much more difficult than it sounds when you're trailing a drip and stand.

I had not suffered from the raging thirst that often accompanies the onset of diabetes, but as soon as they put me on that drip, I was emptying my water carafe within minutes. I have never felt so dried out, and just poured water down my throat as if my insides were a roaring furnace that needed quenching and extinguishing. Very strange!

After the twenty-four hours, my friend in adversity had managed about half a litre whereas I was on my fifth. I know how a hose feels now, with water being fed in one end and just passing out the other, with no apparent time delay between the two actions.

We had a special diabetic diet which contained so much food that I couldn't possibly eat it. Any food left was a scolding offence, so I took to hiding chunks of bread in my locker in case I got night starvation. It was, however, healthy and edible food, something I would have been more grateful for, had I had a crystal ball, and could have seen what things would be like during two future stays there.

Normal daily medication was taken over by the hospital staff, and I take Warfarin daily because of a blood clotting disorder. As I have had four DVTs (Deep Vein

Thromboses), my therapeutic range, measuring the thickness of my blood, is higher than normal, and I tried as hard as I could to explain this to an incredibly arrogant young doctor. He, though, realised that I was a mere woman, English, to boot, and therefore inferior, and ignored what I said, dosing me as he thought fit.

After the first day of this dosage I began to panic, because my last DVT had been while I was actually taking Warfarin, and was the reason I had a higher dosage than Dr Arrogant thought necessary. When we moved here, we bought a little machine with which I could test my own blood, and I asked Ian to bring it in the next day, which would be after two days of inadequate dosage.

For two days, we tested and recorded the rapidly falling results. When my next hospital test was done, I asked to be informed of the result, which very closely matched that of my own machine. I also got Ian to bring in my record book, which stated my therapeutic range in the front. I'd already had one run in with Dr Arrogant who'd stated that the consultant had set the dose, and the consultant could not possibly be wrong. After all, she was an experienced consultant, and I was just a (foreign) patient. Doctors still have this god-like status in France.

A kind nurse provided me with the lab result from my blood test and, with my treatment book in my hand and my trusty testing machine shining out the result, I summoned Dr Arrogant and presented him with the evidence. I then managed to make him understand that I had suffered on four previous occasions with deep vein thrombosis, and he crumbled, especially when I informed him that he might be about to kill me with a fifth. My dosage was increased forthwith, and he avoided me for the rest of my stay on the ward. My house-point, I believe! And now I think of him as Dr Shifty.

FRONT DOOR BLUES

While I was incarcerated in the hospital, Ian had started the process of getting quotes, they are called *devis* here, for a new front door. The door was a collection of miscellaneous very old planks and nails with holes in so big that a dog could get in, not to mention birds, which were actually nesting in the hall. When we first arrived, Ian nailed various bits of wood over the bigger holes and stapled cardboard over all the gaps he could in an attempt to keep out the cold. While that effectively failed, being able to see your breath in the hall every day until the weather warmed up, it was at least better than being completely open to the elements.

Now, we are opposite a church which is designated an ancient monument, so we knew that we would have to have the door sympathetically replaced. In France, anywhere within 500 metres of a designated monument has to abide by very strict rules about changes to its appearance. The old double doors were horizontal oak planks fixed together with handmade domed head nails. Ian reckoned that the door was at least two hundred years old and it looked the same as the front door on the church.

So we needed a bespoke door with an upper fanlight in oak and we wanted it to have the nailed effect. We started the search for a supplier.

The first was an expat whose name was given to us by one of the builders. He showed up in a scruffy white British-registered van and with no official business registration (it was going through as we spoke apparently!), a common thing here, and commenced to suck his teeth loudly – if I'd only had dentures I'd have offered those for him to suck as well – and began scribbling on an old envelope. He then said he wanted cash only, again a common thing with ex-pats, nudge nudge, wink wink, we didn't want to give Sarkozy too much tax!

Ian said he would want references and some pictures of previous work done by him. Not surprisingly we didn't hear from him again.

Our rather eccentric neighbour Jean-Marc Rubio was taking a keen interest in what we were up to at the house and would often stop on his way past and have a word and a quick look. On one of these frequent visits, Ian had mentioned that he was looking to replace the front doors and Jean-Marc got very excited and said he knew a man who could do a fantastic job for us who was very interested in the historical integrity of old buildings. He contacted him for us and this chap duly arrived. He went by the fantastic name of Leo Gwizdala – not an obviously French name – and looked like a hippy. He was a *menuisier-ébeniste* which means carpenter and cabinetmaker and a small alarm bell started to ring in Ian's head. They discussed the job and Leo was very enthusiastic about this 'project', more alarm bells, and really got into the swing of how he would replicate the existing door, even proposing to re-use the old hand-made nails. Needless to say Leo spoke fairly good English or Ian would not have had a clue what he was saying. After a long chat, a look at his portfolio which included a lot of fancy stuff, clang clang, and a glass of red wine, he left promising to present his proposals in the near future. When we got his *devis* we nearly fainted, it was well over five thousand euros! Too rich for our blood.

The third chap was a Frenchman recommended by our neighbour Gerard. Now he was very French and didn't speak a word of English, and arrived with what turned out to be his daughter, who had a few words but was painfully shy and looked slightly incongruous in her dungarees. So it turned out to be Monsieur Laprade and daughter, not son! They went about measuring with lots of incomprehensible (to us) Gallic muttering and noting down things in a very comforting professional manner.

After some further discussions and a lot of sign language and general waving of arms, M Laprade declared that he had enough information and went off to make his *devis*. This one turned out to be just under three thousand euros, which happened to be the budget that we had set for the door. We contacted them and agreed the price and asked them when they could start. After a pause he said *février*, that's February isn't it? Surely we had misunderstood, it was only September. In a panic at the thought of another winter with the old door, we asked if we could have priority. *Vous avez la priorité maintenant* came back! Reluctantly we agreed as we were desperate to resolve the issue and steeled ourselves for another freezing winter in the house.

CHAPTER ELEVEN

Lost in France; The Outlaws have a stab at seeing me off; The hospital makes a second attempt on my life

LOST IN FRANCE

I came out of hospital at the end of the first week in October to find that, in my absence, my husband's parents had decided to come a-visiting with his Auntie Mary and his grandmother. Although they had booked into a *chambre d'hôte* (bed and breakfast), this would still mean a lot of work for me, for although the place they were staying did evening meals on request, I would still be feeding them for some of the time and making sure that, whatever stage the work on the house was at, the rest of it was scrupulously clean and tidy, for my mother-in-law is a fiend for cleanliness.

I did feel that it was a very inconsiderate time to visit, seeing that I would only have been out of hospital for three days, but then, they were never people who actually considered other people's wishes, when making plans for what they wanted to do, and when they wanted to do it.

With the treatment I had received, though, and my new medication regime for controlling the diabetes, I found I had a lot more energy than I'd had for months, and that the numbness had disappeared from my legs, retreated down my feet, and now affected only my toes, so I did feel a little more up to the occasion.

Ian had lived with his grandmother for quite a lot of his formative years, and I was really looking forward to seeing her. She was a lovely lady of ninety-four, very spry and nimble on her feet and definitely in possession of every one of her marbles. She was a pleasure to talk to, and fascinating to listen to when she told tales about the family's past. Born at the beginning of the First World War, she had some fascinating stories to tell, not the least of which was the tragedy of her early years, about which I had never known before.

Ian made an arrangement, as they were coming via the Channel Tunnel and driving down, that if his father could get as far as the nearest town, he would meet them there in the main car park and lead the way to our home. They had been there, very briefly, when we viewed the place in May 2007, but were not in the least interested in walking round what they saw as 'just another wreck', so went for a little walk while we were guided round, falling more in love with the place with every step we took.

The saga of them getting here started about half an hour before Ian was expecting David to call to say that they had arrived in the car park. They had not. They were lost somewhere we could not identify, because of David's pronunciation. He'd never studied French and had an accent straight out of *Auf Wiedersehen Pet*.

We eventually identified his location as Angoulême, a town notoriously easy to get lost in; we'd done it ourselves on one of our trips here by car. Ian asked if he had a satnav. No! Did he have a map book? Yes. Where was it? In the boot!!!

Three more phone calls still identified them as lost in Angouleme, and I can only assume that they pulled over to the side of the road to throw three double sixes, to earn a 'Get Out of Angouleme Free' card, for they did eventually arrive in the nearby town, to be led back here, very much later than expected.

After a quick look round, Ian then led them to their *chambre d'hôte* and asked his father to take note of the route from our house, because he would need to reverse the route in order to visit us the next day. He had already pointed out to him that if he missed the turning off the D13, he would know he'd done it within a hundred yards, because he would pass a cemetery on his right, and that would be the indication that he'd overshot his turning.

We waited with them while they booked in and were shown their rooms, and then the moaning started. They had booked three rooms and, each one of them, with the exception of Nan, seemed jealous of one of the others' room. The squabbling was like a group of toddlers feeling hard done by over who was playing with which toy. Eventually we left them to it, made arrangements for them to come over to our house the next day, and went home, grateful for the silence.

The following day, the appointed hour for them to arrive came and went, and we'd received no phone call to say that they were delayed. Where were they? How could they have got lost? It was a very straightforward route, with no awkward bits in it. Even I could have driven it, had I the guts to drive on what I considered to be the wrong side of the road.

They arrived about forty-five minutes late, David in a cross fluster, the three ladies looking rather more relaxed. David immediately went out into the garden to inspect it, and to calm down. While he was outside, Nan explained that they had gone almost to Echourgnac, having passed the cemetery about eight kilometres before.

'But you knew he'd passed it?' I asked.

'Of course I did,' Nan replied. 'But he's always so certain he knows everything, and won't listen to anyone else, that I didn't bother to say anything.'

'I saw the cemetery, too,' said Auntie Mary.

Brenda said nothing, you could see in her eyes that she had seen it too, but kept her lip firmly buttoned.

While they were here, we went out for the day together to a beautiful historic town called Brantôme. It is on a river, and is picture-postcard perfect. We wandered round there for a couple of hours, then went down near the river to a restaurant for lunch.

The menus were only in French, so I offered David the handy little dictionary I carry everywhere we go. He, however, refused, and said he'd seen steak on the menu, and that's what he would have. I hadn't noticed any steak, but forbore to comment, as he was so know-it-all, that I would be wrong.

Ian had ordered snails for his starter, at which point his father had turned ashen under his all-year-round tan and grimaced. His son was evidently into this foreign stuff, but he wasn't having any of that. He had ordered a good old-fashioned reliable steak.

When his own plate arrived, it became clear to both Ian and me that he fallen for a trap for the unwary, and ordered *steak haché*, which is a burger. It was served with chips, salad garnish, and had a beautifully fried egg on top.

He blew his stack, especially when he cut into the fat meat patty and found it to be what I would describe as medium rare. Where the hell was his steak? He'd ordered it, and they'd brought him this muck.

Trying to restrain my mirth, I explained that *steak haché* was French for a burger. If he'd only used the dictionary, he would have known this before he ordered. I cut into it and tried a bite. It was delicious, being a hundred per cent beef, which is typical for France – none of the muck they put into cheap burgers in England.

He was, however, inconsolable and furiously embarrassed, although he wouldn't order anything else, pushed the burger to the side of his plate as though it were a piece of doggy do-do and went into sulk mode.

As Ian and I ordered dessert and coffee, David practically dragged Brenda away from the restaurant, went to the shop at the corner, and flagrantly purchased two Cornettos. His loss, I thought, not ours. He is a man who simply will not ask for information, as he considers he knows everything and shouldn't need to enquire anything of other people.

As they had decided to eat at the *chambre d'hôte* that night, Ian led them to a tiny roadway off to the right, on our way home. He had explained that, if his father drove about four hundred yards down that and turned right, that would shortly turn into the drive of where they were staying, and it would only take them a few minutes to get back. It was just a little memory jog, in case he had forgotten the route in his paddy at lunch earlier.

We drove home, and about half an hour later the phone rang and it was him. 'Where are you?' Ian asked, puzzled that they were not back in their rooms.

'In that supermarket car park in the town,' he replied.

'Why?'

'I don't know why. I just am.'

'How the dickens did you get there?'

'I don't know. I followed your instructions.'

Oh no he hadn't. Ian dutifully drove off to find them, then led them back to where they were staying. It would have been difficult for any driver to have gone more wrong over such an easy route, with only one turn off.

THE OUTLAWS HAVE A STAB AT SEEING ME OFF

On the last night of their stay, they invited us over to their *chambre d'hôte* to eat there – their treat – and I thought it would be nice to be cooked for, for a change. How naïve I was. If only I'd known then what I know now, and all those other clichés about hindsight that we always recite when things go disastrously wrong.

The first course was very large whole prawns, of which Ian and I are both inordinately fond, and I took the tail off my first one and took an enthusiastic bite. Right, now for the head, I thought, pulling at it. It came away, dark brown ichor pouring on to the plate. That was definitely not right, and I summoned the owner.

'*Zut alors! Je suis désolée!*' she shrieked, taking away the plate (destroying the evidence, in my opinion), evidently glad that we were the only diners that evening. I don't remember the rest of the meal, because I couldn't get this picture out of my head of what had poured onto my plate.

Ian's parents left early the next morning. The day after they left, I was back in hospital, in agony, and suffering from food poisoning which had also triggered diverticulitis. I would rather give birth without any pain relief, than go through again what I did in the day after they fled back to England in all innocence (I assume!).

It was very lucky that I could not even entertain the thought of eating anything, for the food this time on a different ward, was a fibre-free and sugar-free diet. To say that the hospital food was appalling would be too much of a compliment to it. I think I would have been more prepared to eat a dog-shit sandwich than the absolute garbage they passed off as food, three times a day, in my room.

When I was feeling a little more human (and hungry), I did get very upset, telling the nurse that the food was inedible. Her retort was typical of the nursing staff in that particular hospital. 'You will 'ave to go 'ungry, then,' she snapped, and left the room, slamming the door behind her. (I should say that I'm sure there is excellent healthcare in France, indeed some friends have had very good experiences, but my own personal experience has not been great.)

I eventually got Ian to bring me in snacks and food that I knew were okay on the diabetic diet, but I lost a considerable amount of weight during that period (alas, now found and re-attached, along with some of its friends).

THE HOSPITAL MAKES A SECOND ATTEMPT ON MY LIFE

While I was in there, I was attached to the inevitable drip, this time with fluid so that I didn't get dehydrated, antibiotics to combat the food poisoning, and a strong painkiller so that I didn't spend twenty-four hours a day in agony.

I was in a room of my own this time, and it meant I could read as late as I wanted to, and belch and pass wind without any embarrassment or apology. That may seem a small freedom, but believe me, I really appreciated it. It's not easy being imprisoned in a room with a stranger, round the clock.

Ian, bless him, came in twice a day, as he had done when I was in there only the previous month. He also rang me between visits, so that I didn't lose the will to live. I was beginning to feel like a professional patient, and never wanted to see this place again once I'd been discharged. Silly, silly me! That was a red rag to the Bull of Fate, wasn't it?

One evening, a nurse came round to change my drip bags and, when she'd gone, I began to feel very faint. I looked at the bags hooked up to my vein and realised that one of them was already half-empty. That couldn't be right, could it? And it was rushing through the tube like it was trying to reach the sea. As I watched this happening, I became so faint that I nearly passed out.

Immediately pressing the bell to summon help, I grabbed the offending tube and bent it over, to stop the relentless flow of whatever was in that bag into my arm. I was now lying on the bed trying to stay conscious.

The nurse arrived, and I tried to explain to her that what I had identified as the pain killer was flowing into my vein much too fast, and that I had been on the point of losing consciousness when I had bent over the tube. She was absolutely furious! How dare I do such a thing, and I was to let go immediately. The doctor had prescribed whatever was in the bag, and I had no right to question the doctor – see what I mean about the attitude to doctors here?

Now, I've been caught out with this intravenous liquid business, years before in an English hospital, when I was receiving Heparin by vein. The bag had been changed last thing before lights out, I went to sleep, and the next thing I knew, the lights were on, and I was surrounded by medical staff saying, 'Don't worry! We have the antidote!' Someone – who was never identified to me, the victim – had not mixed the drug with sufficient fluid, and I'd been overdosing while I slept.

And here I was again, now in a French hospital, being overdosed on pain killers, which could prove lethal. The nurse and I tussled verbally until she made a grab for the tube, to stop me bending it, and I made a grab for the cannula in my vein, threatening to pull it out, if something wasn't done immediately about my complaint.

Eventually she gave up, summoned the duty doctor, and received fresh instructions. When she returned, though, she had two bags, which she hooked up to my tube. I was too woozy to even think about it, and just grateful that I'd noticed before I'd become unconscious. When she left, however, I began to feel worse than I had before, with a feeling of slipping away from reality stealing over me. What exactly did she have in her extra little bag?

It was only bloody Valium! I complained, because I was being over dosed with painkiller, and the doctor had evidently instructed her to knock me out with Valium, so that I didn't cause either her or the nurse any further trouble. Just remembering this makes me speechless with disbelief, that it actually happened in the twenty-first century, in a so-called civilised country.

The next night, when the nurse came to renew my bags,

Ian was on the phone, and while we were talking, I noticed that there was a fourth bag about to be attached again. Alarm bells immediately rang in my head, as I asked what was in the fourth bag. Would you believe that it was Valium AGAIN!

I told Ian on the phone that I was about to be sedated against my will which, in my opinion, constituted assault, and that he was a telephonic witness. If she tried to put that stuff into me again, she was going to have to physically fight me.

'Ze docteur says you must 'ave eet,' stated the nurse, as if God himself had issued a new commandment.

I was not rude. I was not violent. I was just firm. I didn't 'ave eet! I was, however, branded a troublemaker for the rest of my stay on that ward. Little did I know that 2009 would see me back there, experiencing the casual cruelty and utter disregard for patients' dignity and feelings that the nurses here could display, but that's another story.

CHAPTER TWELVE

Television; The opening of a new library; More wood already; The great chutney disaster of 2008; Never believe anybody when it comes to insurance

TELEVISION

Since we arrived here, we have neither been able to receive, nor have had time, to watch any television, either French or English but – great excitement – a man is coming to plumb us in, and we shall be able to goggle again at the inanities that the magic box in the corner has to offer, and not long before Christmas.

We have survived, so far, should we need to do a bit of flopping, by watching what I recorded on to DVD before we left the UK. I worked my little cotton socks off (oh, I do love a good cliché or ten) and had recorded over a thousand hours, thus ensuring that, if we never had television reception again, we should be adequately entertained well into our dotage. We had also spent many a happy hour in companionable silence, just reading.

What excitement, though, to see something that was on NOW, and not over a year ago. It was great to be able to keep up with the news again, as neither of us ever manages to concentrate enough to listen to the radio, and out of date English newspapers here cost an absolute fortune.

I had even survived giving up soap operas, and felt not the slightest inclination to tune in to either *Coronation Street* or *Emmerdale*. After all this time, I'd probably not recognise any of the cast members, the turnover in recent years seeming to have been very fast.

What a load of old tripe it really is with, here and there but very few and far between, some absolute gems. We made a pact just to stick to these, but there were so few of them that we had to let a little trash back into our lives, and when we only wanted to throw ourselves on the sofa and 'lard', it was thoroughly satisfying to watch something that was so unimportant that we didn't have to concentrate very hard and could just chill.

THE OPENING OF A NEW LIBRARY

What was much more exciting was the fact that our new bedroom was ready for us to move into, and we could now sleep behind double-glazing in an insulated room. What bliss! Of course, we had to paint it and the en-suite first, but we were eager, and we can paint very quickly when we want to, without doing a crap job.

That was one advantage of having investment properties in the UK. When we bought them, we had to get them looking smart and ready to rent as soon as possible because, just because we didn't have a tenant in, didn't mean that the mortgage would suddenly go away for a month or two.

We kept the palette unobtrusive and painted the new en-suite in white and the bedroom in magnolia, so that it was the things that we put in the rooms that gave them their character.

We also had to build wardrobes as we had built-in ones in four out of the five bedrooms in the old house, and the ones we had brought with us were now ensconced in the two guest bedrooms in the other upstairs wing.

We had purchased two from a rather useful shop in Perigueux called BUT, and they had been delivered in flat-pack form while I was in hospital. They had been sitting leaning up against a wall in the library for some time now, while we did all the painting. It would be much more sensible to assemble them after this job was done, and it was a necessary one because, once they were built, there was no way they could be brought out of the bedroom without taking them apart again. They were very large, and had mirrored doors for practical purposes.

A day or two before we were due to do this job, I took a look at them, and realised there was no 'them' about it. There was far too little there for it to be both wardrobes. I called Ian and he checked, and I was right. They had delivered only one, and that had been weeks ago. What to do?

He had to ring the store and see if they could lay their hands on this missing wardrobe, because we were under the impression that we had bought the two that were the last of the line. If they couldn't find it, we were absolutely in the proverbial, because we'd never be able to get another matching one.

They phoned back a couple of hours later and said that they had found it in their stock room, and when would we be able to take delivery. Very sorry about that. So would we have been, if they had sold it to someone else, not realising that it had been left behind, and was not for sale any more. Phew!

They were hell to assemble, but we eventually finished the job and moved our bed, chest of drawers and tallboy from our previous quarters, and the whole thing was up and running, as far as going up the wooden hill to Bedfordshire was concerned. And it was no time at all before it was a pleasure instead of a torture to go upstairs at night.

That left us with the library to do. As with the bedroom, we had to start with waxing the new floorboards. What a foul job that is, if you don't have rubber knees, but we worked as fast as we could with a large tin of wax each, and a cloth that got more and more disgusting as we worked.

When that was finally done, we took a long hard look at our completely empty library, now clear of ladders, floodlights, and miscellaneous tools. God, it looked big: sixty square metres of absolute emptiness that now needed to be painted three times, for good coverage.

I don't know if you're familiar with French paint, but it's slightly more watery than milk, and costs slightly more than gold. And we had the ceiling to do too, as well as the stairwell and hall, which were all really just one big job.

We have a division of labour that works really well for us when painting. Ian does the top bits while I do everything from the floor up to about six feet. As I paint at a ferocious pace, this keeps us nicely together, albeit on different sides of a room, so that we finish virtually simultaneously, and the job is done. We painted as if our lives depended on it, and finished the first coat in a day. That, being undercoat and therefore akin to skimmed milk, was dry by the next morning, and we started all over again, yelling such fascinating questions at each other, such as: 'Can you see if I've done this bit? I can't remember, and I can't see from this angle.'

The second coat took slightly longer to dry, because we were up to the real milk of French topcoat now, so we took a day off on day three. So anxious were we to finish, though, that we were back at it on day four, finally finishing it in early evening, covered in paint and absolutely exhausted. We had used seventy litres of paint between us, on this mammoth task, and they hadn't been cheap. Unfortunately, on our last trip over, we hadn't known what a good idea it would be to go to a DIY store and stock up.

It was done, though, and within a few days we could start bringing the boxes of books up from the barn. We'd already measured, estimated, and decided that we'd need thirteen tall bookcases to house our books, and had ordered them from IKEA in a glorious bright red colour.

Willing to pay the delivery charge, for once, they were to be delivered in a couple of days, and then Operation Library could really begin. And guess who the librarian was. You've got it. Me!

Putting together the bookcases was a doddle after the first one, and we were knocking them off in about fifteen minutes each, once we got into the swing of it. What a difference that made, putting them all in position. Ian had been unsure about the brightness of the colour, but we both decided that we LOVED the red. It was just so shouty and loud and happy.

Ian now became box deliverer, and I the box emptier. It might seem the absolute pits to some people to have so many books to sort, and then put in order, on that number of shelves, but I'm a weird little chore-monkey, and really love sorting things and putting them away in a tidy fashion. They went in alphabetically, category by category, and I felt happier and happier as the shelves filled up.

There would be no more wanting to re-read, or look at a book, and realise that it was still in the boxes in the barn and hadn't made it into bookery-nook, which was now a thing of the past. We had packed up our books a year ago, and I'd missed them dreadfully. Now I could be reunited with all my old paper friends, and I worked as fast as I could to make this a reality.

We also had to put some furniture in that huge space, and luckily I had persuaded Ian that we just *had* to buy a pair of red sofas, and one of those chairs with the matching footstool, all financed out of the illegal 'miscellaneous fund' in the refurbishment money. With the other furniture from our old house we had already allocated for this room, and the rugs that we had ear-marked for it, it looked an absolute delight when it was all put together, and I'm still proudest of that room in our house, because it was completely my vision.

MORE WOOD ALREADY

It only seemed like a few weeks ago that we had our first delivery of wood, and here we were again, needing more. Last time we had bought from Paul's supplier and not been entirely happy. This time Gerhard had recommended the farmer who supplied him, and whom he had used for years. We took his advice, as Gerhard is a real wood nut, and likes to keep his barn stacked with enough logs to see him through another war (only kidding!)

When it arrived, not only was it not just dumped in a heap on the drive, but delivered in bound bundles of a steer (one cubic metre), all exactly the same size, and unloaded by crane, right outside the entrance to the wood barn. It was also cheaper.

When Ian stacked it in the barn, he commented on the fact that there was no rotten wood at all, and that it took up a lot more space than the exact same amount we had purchased from the other guy! We would definitely stick with our new supplier. Paul, as usual, had his dumped in a huge heap at the road end of his drive, blocking his way in and out with the car, until it had been moved. *Danke schön*, Gerhard! Nobody likes being done over, and the previous supplier would not get another chance to put one over on us again!

THE GREAT CHUTNEY DISASTER OF 2008

We knew we'd made a great deal of chutney, pickles, and jams. As far as the chutney went, I'd stopped keeping a record of how much we made when it got over 60lbs. All of this largesse went into a wall cupboard in the business bit of the barn.

We know it was stupid, now. We knew the kitchen cupboards had been in use for about seven years in our old garage, during which time they'd been overloaded with store cupboard food. Isn't it weird how incapable you become of putting two and two together, if no one actually instructs you to use your fingers on which to count?

It happened just after Paul and Denise had given us a hand putting the wood away, as we had done a similar favour for them, so that they could get their car out.

There was this almighty crash, as if the end of the world had happened, only inside our barn and not over the whole planet. Ian was the first on the scene, and uttered a despairing, 'Oh, no!' I rushed to where he was standing with his mouth open, and surveyed the remains of our hoard.

The whole cupboard had pulled itself off the wall, scattering bottles and jars as it went, and broken glass, jam, chutney and an awful lot of pickled gherkin chunks now ranged over the floor in a flood of vinegar. Not only had the whole cupboard collapsed and fallen off the wall, but it had landed on our brand new chest freezer which was sitting just below it, and put a hefty dent right across the lid. We can never keep anything looking new for long, and this was just about (cliché coming up) par for the course.

On closer examination, it wasn't quite so bad as it had first seemed, and many of the fruits of our labours were intact, and able to be moved into a new cupboard – and not one mounted on the wall this time. Of course, it took an awful lot of clearing up, and that section of the barn smelled of pickles for some considerable time after, but at least we hadn't lost the entire contents of our store cupboard, although we had actually lost the cupboard itself, which was now fit only for the tip.

There's a moral to this tale, I think, and that moral is: chutney has no head for heights, so always store it where it doesn't have far to fall.

NEVER BELIEVE ANYBODY WHEN IT COMES TO INSURANCE

When we moved in, we were aware that there was a large crack in the barn wall on the western side. We were informed by the vendor that it had happened in the drought of 2005, and would be covered by her insurance, as it had been declared a national disaster, and the government had underwritten damage resulting from this extreme weather.

When we had signed for the property in the *notaire*'s office, the *notaire* herself had also assured us that the claim had been registered and agreed, and we were given a piece of paper with an estimate for over fifteen thousand euros on it, to remedy the damage to the structure. We were happy that all this could be sorted out when we were ready, although we didn't understand anything but the figures on the insurance document.

Ian was now ready, and contacted the insurance company about getting started on the work, and claiming back the money. THAT was when the real truth emerged.

The previous owner had only insured it as a holiday home. Her cover was, therefore, not comprehensive, and the most that they were willing to pay us was about three thousand euros. She knew this, as she was the one who'd insured it. The *notaire* must have known this too, if she was doing her job properly in dealing with *all* the paperwork, this insurance document included. We'd been shafted again!

If it were really to cost that much, and we could expect no more than three thousand euros, then that would definitely have to be put off for another day, for funds were running very low, and it was time to reassess our financial situation in the light of the work still to be completed, before it could be left for another phase, when we had, somehow, replenished the coffers.

We'd already tried to sell one of our apartments in the

UK, but the market was even worse than when we sold our house, and it was a non-starter from the first. What with the ferocious drop in property prices, we'd be lucky to clear the mortgage on it and pay legal fees. At least it had a tenant at the moment and wasn't costing us anything, so we decided to stick with the status quo in that respect, and see what life presented to us in the future.

CHAPTER THIRTEEN

We just can't afford the staff, these days; A very English carol party; Singing in the Abbey; In the bleak midwinter; First Christmas without a crowd; Long John Turkey; Looking to the future

WE JUST CAN'T AFFORD THE STAFF, THESE DAYS

After a long struggle with the bleedin' obvious, we decided that we would have to let Beeny go, because, well and hard as he'd worked, everything that absolutely had to be finished off was in Barney's range of expertise, and he was a damned quick worker, taking only twenty to thirty minutes for lunch, and being liable to work well beyond his allotted daily time without charging a centime extra, and always arrived bang on the dot every morning. If we had any chance of achieving what we needed to, it was with him.

It was very sad to end our professional association with Beeny, but we had no choice. It wasn't long, however, until this was completely driven out of our heads by the next thing that happened. Monkey disappeared again.

This time I knew it was for good. It was a Sunday, and we wondered if she'd been shot by one of the hunters. A friend of hers had her cat shot, actually in her garden, by an over-zealous hunter. There was no sign of my darling, though, when Ian searched the woods. He even walked all the local roads to see if she'd been hit by a car, but there was not a trace.

Me? I still believe she was stolen. She was super-friendly and would have been curious enough to get into a strange vehicle and socialise with complete strangers. I really can't write about this as it is still too painful.

A VERY ENGLISH CAROL PARTY

I had decided that it would be a great idea if we invited all the new friends we had made to a carol party *chez nous*. We had made about a stone of mincemeat earlier in the year, and we could buy sausage meat at the supermarket, these being the days before we started making our own sausage meat, sausages and faggots.

We could provide a heavy load of mince pies (home-made of course) and the same of sausage rolls, and Ian could make a vat of mulled wine, and I could play all the carols on the digital piano with it in pipe organ mode. We could produce the invitations on the computer, and I could give them out at choir, and we could stick the local ones in people's mail boxes.

I diligently checked with everyone whether they were going back to the UK for Christmas, and when, then we decided on a date for the party. It should be great fun with a mixture of English and French, and get us all in the festive mood for later in the month, when there were several more musical things to do.

The choir would be singing for the Nine Lessons and Carols service at Chancelade Abbey, and then, just a couple of days before Christmas itself, performing outdoors under the outdoor market halls in a rather far-away town, for anyone who wanted to come along and listen, or join in for a jolly good singsong. We'd be first, though, while everyone still had maximum enthusiasm.

The day before the party, Ian scoured the garden for suitable greenery with which to drape the two pianos in the dining room and we put up a tree; something we wanted to leave as close to the event as possible because, although we only had one cat left, we knew he was no angel, and dangling Christmas tree baubles are irresistible to the feline species.

The day of the party was a harum-scarum day of baking, sorting out suitable drinking vessels for hot wine, copying sheets with the words of the carols on, so that everyone could join in with more than the first verse, and practising like crazy, so that I didn't make too much of an idiot of myself on the piano. I hate playing in public!

When I was a teenager (and quite a promising pianist, then), I arrived for one show very under-rehearsed, and actually walked out of the hall in the middle of my performance, because I was so disgusted with the noise I was producing. Similarly, at the start of all my practical exams, I had to be calmed down, so that my hands would stop shaking sufficiently to allow me to play at all.

I couldn't even play in front of Ian until we'd been married twenty-five years, although I suffered no trouble whatsoever when teaching. During lessons, I was as patient and relaxed as it was possible to be. Mrs Black must have a counterpart in Mrs White, for I am not normally a patient person but, during teaching sessions, a strange peace floods through me, and I become another person altogether.

But, back to the last-minute practising. I knew I wouldn't get away with absolutely no mistakes because these aforementioned nerves (which only involved playing the piano, however, and no other instrument) would ensure I didn't give a perfect performance. The only trick I'd learnt over the years was to carry on as if nothing had happened, hoping that maybe nobody had noticed the wrong notes.

While I hammered away against my greatest enemy, nerves, Ian got on with the production of eight litres of mulled wine. Our German friends had very kindly sent us boxes of *Glühwein* sachets so he had the right flavouring, and he also prepared the sliced fruit that would go into our giant soup pot with the fragrant liquid. Knowing that our neighbour didn't touch alcohol, we had also thought to provide alternatives to this hot and spicy brew, and we knew her husband would whisper a request for a wee tot of whisky. How the French love their Scotch!

The first guests to arrive were the farming family from behind our house, who were half an hour early. Aargh! And not a word of English between them! We'd been well and truly bounced. An easy solution was found, though, just by taking them round the house to see the changes since the previous owner had left and we'd taken on the task of bringing it back to life.

From seven o'clock onwards there was a constant stream of people arriving and an ever-growing pile of coats in the drawing room, which we refer to as the *séjour*, as this is how our neighbours always referred to it.

The dining table was laden with plates and platters of mince pies with our own special ingredient. On the top of each pile of mincemeat, before putting on the tops, we had placed a teaspoonful of home-made plum and cinnamon jam. Oh, the difference! I've never tasted better mince pies. Other plates were piled high with sausage rolls. It really had been a food factory *chez nous* today. The aroma of mulled wine drifted in from the kitchen-cum-everything room, and Christmas carols were softly playing in the background – a CD, not a terrified me.

After everyone had arrived, we let our guests get a few glasses down their necks and have a good old gossip, then I called the proceedings to order while Ian handed out the carol sheets. Our first set for the evening went down a bomb, with the guests even dividing into pages and king for Good King Wenceslas, which turned out to be a favourite of all.

I had my carol file marked-up with the order in which I would play the carols and, shortly after we had begun,

Andrew Chandler took up my flute and began to play along with the melody, switching to descants where appropriate. One of the choir members also asked if we had a book that provided harmonies, and we got a really good sound, with the choir members joining in with the parts they knew by heart, and looking over the hymn books I had hunted out, to swell the singing with alto, tenor and bass, and descants on last verses.

Well exercised of lung and heart, we took a break for a little sustenance, more wine and a good old natter of self-congratulation. Finally, I called everyone back together again, providing the simple percussion instruments I had collected over time – jingle stick, tambourine etc. – and we started afresh, this time Andrew playing along from a hymn book on the other piano.

I had my digital piano set on pipe organ and, with Andrew playing along on the baby grand (a quite odd combination of sounds, as the piano hadn't been tuned since we moved) and, with the addition of the percussion, we made a sound rousing enough to raise the rafters. The party broke up at quite a reasonable hour, as the next day was Friday and some of the guests had work, but we had had long enough to thoroughly welcome Christmas into our minds and hearts and, let's face it, the first carol singing session is always the best.

Both Barney and Beeny had been there with their wives, Beeny's wife arriving like an icicle, because we had had to terminate her husband's time working for us, but she thawed as the evening progressed, and the last few guests who sat around with us chewing the fat and putting the world to rights after everyone else had gone, were these four.

The party had been a much greater success than we could have hoped for, and we resolved to do this every year, if we were able. Our French neighbours, all five of them, had been fascinated to try mince pies, as these are a very English seasonal sweetmeat, and delighted that the mulled wine (and Scotch) were so freely on tap. All the friends we had made in our first year had been there, and it was a nice way to thank them for their company since we had arrived, and left us feeling that all was well with the world.

SINGING IN THE ABBEY

Makes a change from the shower, I suppose!

It had been requested that the choir should sing at the service of nine lessons and carols in mid-December, and I was delighted at the prospect. We had spent hours rehearsing what we would sing, spending the most time on the lesser-known carols that we would perform for the congregation, as most of us knew our parts in the familiar carols inside-out, from frequent singing over the years.

I am seasonally addicted to *Carols from Kings*, and have not missed a service in more years than I care to remember. To be involved in such a service for our first Christmas in France was a real joy to anticipate.

The Sunday of the service dawned grey and threatening, and bitterly cold. We had been advised to wrap up warmly, as we would have to spend the afternoon in the Abbey rehearsing, then hang around until service time, before singing for real.

I chose a huge mink coat that I'd bought from an internet auction site just before we moved here. It was vintage, and had cost virtually nothing, and I had no qualms on the animal rights side, as the animals had been dead long before I was born. At least they were still providing pleasure (and warmth) for someone.

Being a somewhat cold body (and having experienced -31 degrees on a winter holiday in Quebec) I decided on the ultimate warm headgear, as so much heat is lost through the head. That morning I selected one of my wigs – the grey one that Ian hates so much – and I wore that under a furry hat. No way was I giving up my hard-earned heat to a freezing cold stone building.

The Abbey itself was not large, but it could sure retain the cold. While we rehearsed, our breath made clouds in the air, and we must have resembled a gathering of dragons who could not ignite their fiery breath, as we sent out Christmas praises heavenwards.

The service was not quite as I expected it to be, but then this was France, not King's College, and the pews were full of those who like a little Christ in their Christmas, and not just Slade pop songs and commercialism.

Afterwards mince pies and mulled wine were served to those who had taken the time to come along and, later, as we drove home through the darkness, small flakes of snow began to fall. It couldn't have been more perfect.

IN THE BLEAK MIDWINTER

Just a few days before Christmas, the choir congregated again, this time in a small town about fifty kilometres away from our home, to sing under the ancient market halls, for any residents who had a mind to come along and join in. It was, of course, a nostalgic magnet for the ex-UK residents, although a goodly number of locals also turned up. This was something the choir had done before, but again, it was a first for me.

The weather was bitter, the ground icy, and just standing took quite a lot of concentration. We only did one number for choir only; the rest were the good old-fashioned carols that everyone knew, plus more modern additions such as Jingle Bells and Rudolf the Red-nosed Reindeer (with some verses in French!), and a lovely tenor solo of Chestnuts Roasting on an Open Fire.

A local restaurant across the road kindly let us use their

toilet facilities, and provided mince pies and mulled wine free, for the choir and all those who turned up to join in, a seasonal gesture of real generosity, and entirely in the spirit of the season.

An electricity supply had been jury-rigged and we even had our rehearsal keyboard with us. The strains of this, along with the steam from our mouths, rose upwards in thanks for all that we had, and enjoyed, at this time of year.

FIRST CHRISTMAS WITHOUT A CROWD

We decorated the house nearer to the day with enthusiasm, putting a tree in the library, a tree in the *séjour*, a tree in the dining room (already erected for the carol party), and a tree in the middle room. All our little seasonal ornaments went into the *séjour,* and tinsel was strewn everywhere, so long as it was out of reach of Merlin, our one remaining cat.

We were not in a position to buy presents for each other so, in October, when we had gone to the Phoenix (an animal charity) book sale – an event that sold donated second-hand books at a euro each, to swell coffers – we had both purchased books that we would give to each other. It made no difference that they were pre-owned books: the stories were new to us, and that was all that mattered.

We also had a gift each under the tree from Stephanie & Co, as she had brought them with her when she had visited us in September. Our German friends had also sent us a Christmas parcel, and so we had some things to open that would be a surprise. The one thing that was missing, of course, was family.

Price rises at this time of year for all forms of transport keep families apart, and it kept us apart this year because our children couldn't afford the profiteering prices to visit us, we couldn't afford tickets for them; nor could we afford to go to the UK ourselves. It would have to be a different sort of Christmas, with phone calls our only contact with our loved ones. We did not yet have broadband, and could not even Skype them.

Thankfully, Stephanie had taken over as Mother Christmas, had invited all her siblings and their partners, and would provide the sort of Christmas we've always had as a family, with all our personal traditions reproduced intact. It is something that she still continues to do, to show her love for her family and, next year, we might even be able to join them, to bring us all back together at that most important time of the year.

We did the best we could on our own, but this was an unwelcome first for us. Sometimes, in the middle of all the inevitable squabbling and sheer volume, we had speculated what Christmas would be like on our own, but now we had the opportunity to try it, it wasn't so grand.

Where were the balls of screwed-up wrapping paper all over the floor? Where were the cries of delight, as someone unwrapped something they had been yearning for? Where were the mountains of seasonal food that used to fill our kitchen and utility room? Where was the smell of huge amounts of food cooking for the best meal of the year? Where was all the happiness, the goodwill and, most of all, the laughter and love?

We made the most of what we had, but it felt like there was a huge hole where all the heart should have been. Of the entire year, this was the one time when we desperately missed our children. Christmas simply wasn't Christmas without them.

LONG JOHN TURKEY

The most entertaining bit of the whole Christmas, in retrospect, was coming down on Christmas Eve morning.

A kind friend of a friend had driven over for Christmas and brought us over a turkey. We left it out to defrost when we went to bed on the twenty-third, so that it had plenty of time to thaw before it was cooked.

We went to bed that night without a care in the world, knowing that there were now only two more sleeps till Christmas. The next morning, however, this mood was shattered, when Ian went down first and I heard something akin to a scream as I followed him slowly downstairs.

When I entered the middle room, which had become a French winter sitting room, with kitchen facilities, a dining table, the television and sofas, all sharing the comforts of the one working log-burner in the house, a dreadful sight met my eyes.

The turkey had been left out in its plastic covering, but this had not deterred Merlin, and the flesh (and the plastic) had been completely stripped from one leg. He had also had a merry romp with the Christmas tree in that room, and it was tipped over, with baubles everywhere.

Well, the turkey would just have to have a thorough wash and be cooked as if nothing had happened. We didn't have a substitute, and there was no one sharing our meal to comment on the fact that the bird had teeth marks on it, even before the carving knife had touched it.

When Denise came over shortly after with a card for us, after we had had a reviving cup of coffee, I answered the door with a furious face. 'Whatever's the matter?' she asked, in concern. My reply was succinct and direct.

'We've got Long John Turkey, and the cat's killed the Christmas tree!' I informed her, to her puzzlement. 'Come on in,' I invited, 'and I'll tell you all about it.'

A NEW YEAR

Of course, we got over it – there was no other alternative, and our thoughts turned to the New Year and what 2009 would bring. First, though, we needed to decide whether we would make any new year's resolutions. After much consideration and thought, we decided that the only thing that was absolutely essential was to get some more cats. Merlin was lonely, and the house seemed so empty with just him there on his own.

On the third of January we phoned the Phoenix Association to discover that they had had a kitten of about six months handed in to them just half an hour before. This was fate! Having taken down directions – it was quite a way away – we jumped into the car, full of anticipation and hope.

Would we like her? Would she like us? Would Merlin like her? Tough luck, Merlin, you'll just have to cope, we decided, as we drove down to meet her.

Phoenix does an awful lot of good here. It takes in stray cats and dogs, many of them abandoned by their owners because they're inconvenient, or because they're too expensive or they're bored with them. Many also come from Brits who go back to the UK and just leave their pets behind. Such casual cruelty is beyond our comprehension.

The Association survives on charitable donations and the proceeds of its, now twice a year, sale of second-hand books. It does a marvellous job, and never puts an animal down if it's not absolutely necessary. Foster homes are found, new-born kittens or puppies are fed at two-hourly intervals, and every animal is vaccinated and spayed or neutered, before going to a new home. We salute their sterling efforts and wish them every success with their fund-raising and re-homing.

When we arrived at our destination, we were shown into a room where a kitten sat on the seat of an armchair. She was slate grey, with a white underside and a most intelligent face. We fell in love with her instantly. There was no doubt about whether we would take her. She was ours the moment we set eyes on her. She had been named

Misty when she arrived just over an hour before, and we loved the name as well as the kitten. We were totally kitten-smitten!

The following day we had a call from Phoenix to enquire whether we would consider adopting an older cat who had been in foster care for six months. The thought was certainly worth entertaining, as she sounded as if she really needed a permanent home. She had spent her time in foster care in a large cage, as her foster carer had huge dogs that were not particularly tolerant of cats. We also learnt that she had only a tiny stub of tail, a congenital condition which, had it been a stage further down the line, would have manifested itself as spina bifida.

We made our way, that afternoon, to a small house in the middle of nowhere, with an aviary in the garden, chickens wandering everywhere, very large dogs, and this poor defenceless cat in a cage. Granted, the cage was about the size of a small bedroom in an English house, but it was a cage nevertheless, and it was no life for an animal that needed fresh air and love.

Bless her, she wasn't pretty or cute, and her lack of tail made her look very odd, but how could we leave her there? I had emptied the contents of the purse that contained what I had embezzled from the previous month's housekeeping money, to make a donation for Misty the day before. The donation they wanted for this cat was far more than we could afford.

Of course we came to an agreement and took her, making a donation of something in the region of seventy euros (we'd not eat well in January), named her Madeleine – Maddie for short – and headed off home with her, knowing that Merlin wouldn't be able to believe his eyes when we presented him with yet another cat on, what he had considered, until Misty's arrival yesterday, as his sole territory. Poor Merlin! He's been very long-suffering over the years, but he's never shown his disappointment in us.

Two new heartbeats was a positively excellent way to start a new year in our new home and, as our first anniversary here approached, we knew with absolute conviction that we had done the right thing in our move, whatever the financial consequences. Life was for once only, and, without a bit of adventure and risk, it would not have been fully lived!

Little did we know it, but the future held an awful lot of exciting living, not all of it enjoyable.

CHAPTER FOURTEEN

First tragedy of the year; an unfortunate incident; I am a raspberry; a cavalcade of cats

FIRST TRAGEDY OF THE YEAR

Although Maddie was very standoffish and would not let us pick her up at all, running from our approaches to pet her, Misty was a delightful little animal who loved to play. She was so intelligent that she learnt to pick up a toy in her mouth, if we weren't taking any notice of her. She would then come over to drop it at our feet, looking up with an imploring face. How could we resist her pleading? She was endearing in many ways and really took to Barney when he came back to work in the new year, as our sole builder.

In fact, she became rather too fond of him, and began to howl at him, lower her front, and point her raised rear towards to him. It was a shock to realise that she was offering herself to him, and that she must have been a bit older than Phoenix thought, as she seemed to be in her first season.

An immediate call to the vet sorted out an appointment for her the very next day, and we kept her in until we were able to deposit her with a man who could make sure we weren't inundated with kittens in the near future. She recovered quickly, however, and was soon out on the hunt again.

Misty was particularly endearing when she first woke up. She had fine dark lines at the bottom of her eyes, like ancient Egyptian make-up, and she always was so bleary-eyed, yawning and blinking, that she looked as if she had just awoken with a hangover, and one or other of us couldn't resist picking her up for a cuddle.

It was her daring hunting nature that eventually did for her, though. One day she went out and didn't come back and, when Ian went out to look for her, he found her dead in the middle of the road, just in front of a small derelict building which was a favourite for mousing, and with the mouse she had just killed still in her mouth. It was back to the pampas grass with a spade for Ian, and a very sad day for both of us. We were now down to two cats, neither of which liked to be picked up, and both of which were quite standoffish. This would not do at all. Then, something happened, which completely took our minds off pets for quite a long time.

AN UNFORTUNATE INCIDENT

In February, Gerhard and Ellen came over again for their regular visit and, on their last night here, we went to their house for dinner, coming back shortly after turning into pumpkins and, I reckless fool, suggested we open just another bottle of wine, and sit and have a chat before we went upstairs.

By the time we had finished this, I was thoroughly well-oiled and Ian suggested – in fact, commanded – that I wait at the bottom of the staircase until he had locked up, so that he could help me upstairs, as he didn't consider me too steady on my feet.

Cheeky ornament! I thought and, being allergic to orders, decided to actually run upstairs. Now, apart from my inebriated condition, this was a bad idea for another reason: we still didn't have a handrail attached, and there was absolutely nothing to grab at or hold on to on the way up.

The inevitable took place. Halfway up, I overbalanced

to the right, where a yawning gap down to the tiled floor awaited me, and I fell, landing on my side and head. Of course, Ian came rushing out, making all sorts of: 'You silly bitch, what've you done now?' noises, but he couldn't turn back time.

He knelt down beside me to see what damage I had done, then went very quiet. 'I think I'd better phone for an ambulance,' he said in uncharacteristic worried tones. I never found out until much later that he thought he could see grey matter leaking from my head, and that it was brain tissue and I would surely die.

He kept his mouth shut for now on that one, then returned to say that an ambulance was on its way. They're private here and have to be paid for. I asked him when it would arrive, and he said he hadn't asked. 'Get me a tea towel and the phone,' I demanded and, holding the first to my head as I sat on the floor, I spoke into the other, to ascertain how long they would be.

When the crew and vehicle arrived, I actually walked out to the vehicle, chatting away nineteen to the dozen. At Perigueux hospital, I walked from the ambulance into A&E, and didn't feel too bad at all. There, I had my head looked at, and was put to bed in a double room with a very old Frenchwoman.

Oh boy, was it a different story the next day, when I learnt about – and felt – my injuries, with no alcohol to act as a painkiller. I had a crush fracture of the spine, aforementioned head injury, and four broken ribs, not to mention a whole host of bruising.

I, literally, could not move, and had been catheterised. I could just about lift my head and my arms, but as far as my body and legs were concerned, I was a prisoner on this bed for some time.

The place had not changed, although I was on yet another different ward. As I could not be put into a sitting position to eat, breakfast was a cup of black coffee, lunch was a spouted cup of vegetable soup, and dinner was the same. It was probably the best diet I'd ever been on – one where you can't actually get to any food, and no one brings you anything nutritious.

Perhaps they should try that with people who are morbidly obese and can't get out of bed because their mobility is so restricted by their weight. It certainly worked for me but, remembering the food – muck – I'd been served on my previous stay here, maybe it was me who was the lucky one.

The members of staff, as usual, were as casually cruel as I remembered them and, if the very elderly woman in the next bed rang for a nurse, whoever answered gave her a jolly good shouting at. I felt really sorry for her. It wasn't her fault that she was old and ill, and she had done nothing wrong.

I had to have a body wash every day, and the nurses, two of them in particular, soon worked out how painful it was for me if they turned me over. From then on, they took great delight in my screams of pain, mocking me with great glee. One day they were about this task, and there was a male nurse in the bathroom that was attached to this shared room.

When they got to my private parts, one of the nurses chanted with cruel pleasure, 'Pussy cat, pussy cat.' Her equally sadistic friend joined in, then the male nurse from the bathroom, then they all three had a jolly good laugh at my discomfiture. When they left the room, I had a damned good cry. I felt so humiliated, almost as if I'd been abused.

Ian began to bring me in snacks when he visited, just so that I had something solid to eat. This was much appreciated, as the soup was beginning to get a wee bit monotonous. We did have a big problem, however. I had fallen just two days before our younger daughter, her new partner and our younger son were due to fly out for four days. Now I was a prisoner in hospital again, and I would only see them a couple of times during Ian's visits.

They struck unlucky, of course, when they did get in to see me. The doctor looking after me wanted me to go for a scan of my torso, to confirm the extent of the damage, and moving me from the trolley on to the scanner bed proved so painful that I yelled like a yellow-bellied coward. Then I knew no more.

He had decided on swift and efficient action, and had slipped me a drop of general anaesthetic. The scan caused no further pain, but when I next opened my eyes, I was back in my hospital bed, very bleary-eyed, and being scrutinised by the visiting family as well as my husband.

I was barely conscious, and could not hold a coherent conversation. I looked absolutely dreadful, partly because nobody had bothered to wash my head wound since I had arrived, and there was old, dried blood on a large part of my hair. I barely remember their visit, or the one the next day. I think I may have been suffering slightly from concussion, too. I had certainly ruined their trip over, not just for them, but for me as well, and it was their first time here.

During my stay there, I was measured for a full body brace which, I was told, I would have to wear for three months. Had we not had health cover, the brace would have cost two thousand euros, without fees for the ambulance and hospital stay. We'd have been financially ruined, and would have had to go back to the UK with our tails between our legs.

Anyway, I spent just over a week flat out, then begged to be let home. My brace had been made to measure, and I was told that, if I could walk, I would be allowed home. I was thrilled, until they actually stood me up. The pain was excruciating, even with the brace on, and my bottom and legs felt like they were full of lead.

They said they had to see me walk before they would allow Ian to take me away. I managed to drag myself three steps across the room, and I was dismissed, but how on earth would I manage at home, with stairs to cope with, using the loo, getting in and out of bed and chairs? We would soon find out.

I AM A RASPBERRY

I was now officially a rhyming slang 'raspberry', and life bore no relationship to that which I was living when I was fully mobile. Getting me up or down the stairs took forty-five minutes, as did getting on my brace and clothing in the morning. There was a large piece of metal with a breastplate on said article, which had to be screwed on in the mornings, and unscrewed in the evenings – feel free to make up your own jokes here – and Ian never went up to bed without a screwdriver in his hand.

Going to the loo was a nightmare, especially for my long-suffering husband, as he had to hold my hands to guide my faltering and reluctant steps there, pull down my underwear, hold my hands while he eased me down to a sitting position, and then do everything else involved in the operation, which could not have been pleasant for him, because I certainly couldn't reach round to do the necessary myself. Then reverse the process until I was back safely in my chair.

We devised a system of getting through the days by him getting down the office chair from one of the guest bedrooms. It had wheels, and therefore temporarily functioned as a wheelchair. He then took the lamp off the tall telephone table we had, and put that beside me. I could use that to take coffee and tea, and he placed me in front of the television where I became absolutely hooked on antiques programmes, an interest that was to change my life.

I took meals at the dining table in the middle room, and Ian just pushed me across to it when he served food. It was sheer torture, and a salutary warning to anyone foolish enough to get as rat-arsed as I had done before tackling a staircase at a run. Had there been a handrail, I would undoubtedly have fallen back down the stairs end over end, which could have easily broken my neck. In some ways, I had had a lucky escape, and thoroughly deserved what I was now suffering. This marked a period, lasting a very long time, when I was teetotal, too frightened to drink anything alcoholic.

It was a long and tedious recovery, and the brace now sits on top of a wardrobe in an ornamental capacity, and as a warning to me and anyone else who sleeps in that room, that alcoholic bravado and stairs don't mix.

The interest in antiques, though, sparked off something in my soul, and it wasn't long before Sundays became taken up with visiting car boot sales, quite different here to those in England. We still had hardly any money, so the things I could purchase were very lowly priced, but I became expert at haggling – something I could never have contemplated in my life in the UK. And, what's more, I was doing it in French, so Sunday mornings were not just very cheap shopping opportunities for me, but also French lessons. If I didn't know the name of something I either wanted to look at or buy, I simply asked what the word was in French, and learnt a lot I wouldn't otherwise have picked up from CDs and books.

A CAVALCADE OF CATS

After my slow recovery, we decided that we still didn't have enough cats, especially when the post-lady told us that an old man in the forest had a litter of kittens which had just been born. We immediately asked her to tell him not to drown them, as that was his usual practice, unless someone wanted them.

The next day she told us she had informed him of our

desire to avail ourselves of some of his furry charges, and a date was set to go and view his feline stock.

When we eventually found his house, it was in a very tumbledown state and, when he opened the door to us, the smell hit us full in the face. The mixture of cat urine, human urine, and cat poo almost knocked us flat. We also noticed that the right leg of his trousers was wet to the ankle and discovered, later, via our German friends who knew him well, that he was indeed, incontinent; in fact we were never to see him without this river of urine running down his right trouser leg.

The inside of the house was worse than the outside and, when he offered us coffee, I think both of us nearly passed out with horror. The floor was covered in a sticky layer compounded of urine, dust and general filth and everything was dilapidated and worn out. On the kitchen table in front of his chair was arrayed a collection of bottles and packs of tablets, pills and potions. This was something we had in common, as I recognised some of the things I took myself, and we made a sort of conversation about what we had in common medically.

This was not as easy as it sounds, for not only was he French, but he spoke in patois, which was just about impenetrable for such beginners as us. Eventually, he showed us a cardboard box which contained three beautiful little creatures, one white, one with the beginnings of Siamese-like markings, the other completely ginger. We were in love again, and promptly declared that we would take all three when they were ready to leave their mother.

Before we left, we had the novel experience of watching him feed his cats, for he had six fully grown animals, which bred freely, as the French think it's unnatural to have cats neutered or spayed, rather than cruel to let them give birth to litter after litter and leave them absolutely exhausted and old before their time.

He had very little mobility, although we later found out that he still drove a car and a tractor, and his method, I thought was fairly unique. He simply dropped an enamel plate on the floor from the closest position he could bend to, then poured dry cat food on to it, this, from what passed for his standing position. Cats seemed to come running from every corner and they began to eat immediately. His next move was to pick up a carton of milk and, from the same position he proceeded to pour it in the general direction of the plate. The liquid didn't just moisten the dry cat food, but cascaded over the heads of a couple of feeding animals.

We visited him several times while the cats grew steadily, each time taking him a large bag of dried food, so that he wouldn't be out of pocket keeping the little darlings, for we were sure he would wean them on soggy dry food soaked in milk, and it made us feel better about any extra work they may have caused him.

On the occasion on which we were to pick them up, we took him a bottle of whisky as, apparently, he liked a tipple or two – or three or four. Then, the fun began. The kittens weren't best pleased at being picked up, and escaped off down the hall and into the living room, so we got to see a bit more of the house.

The living room was even worse than the kitchen, with cat poo behind the sofa, behind the log burner, and just about anywhere else that was semi-private. We eventually rounded up all three of them and into a cat basket and, thereafter, always referred to their previous owner as Mr Smelly.

After quite a bit of thought, we called the white one Rasputin, soon shortened by a visiting friend to Ra-Ra, the ginger one Harry, after a certain prince with red hair, and the one with some Siamese in her genetic history, Spud, as she seemed to like sitting on the arm of the sofa watching the television and was, in our eyes, a couch potato. This soon became lengthened to Spudly, by which moniker she is known to this day.

They were such fun but tired easily, finding the best place to fall asleep in a cosy bundle was on my lap, where it was warmest. Harry, unfortunately, wasn't destined for a long life, and he was only a few months old when he died tragically.

Our neighbours, Paul and Denise, had been away and Ian noticed that they had just driven up to their barn. He went across the road to speak to them, as he had been chicken-sitting, and neither of us noticed that Harry had followed him. Ian had only been gone a couple of minutes when there was a furious knocking on the front door and I opened it to find the man from next door who had quite a collection of *chiens de chasse* (hunting dogs) in his back garden.

His face was grave, and so was his message. 'Your cat!' he exclaimed. 'Your cat!' he repeated, indicating for me to follow him, which I did. There, at the bottom of the three steps leading up to the old restaurant entrance on the road side of the house, lay Harry, just twitching his last, with his brains hanging out of his head. Our beautiful ginger cat was dead. He must have followed Ian over, we surmised, then turned round and come home almost immediately, and been caught by a car as he crossed back. We were heart-broken and, once again, Ian began digging in the middle of the crowns of pampas grass.

CHAPTER FIFTEEN

Clay and concrete; back in the hamster wheel again; the smothering coils of bureaucracy; enter an old friend; even more cats

CLAY AND CONCRETE

The part of the barn which had a door into it from the *séjour* had, as I previously mentioned, a very uneven earth floor and, as the weather improved we turned our minds to the arduous task of digging it out and concreting it. We didn't know what we wanted to use it for yet, but it led through to the Jacuzzi and sauna room – the latter not yet re-assembled. At the moment, the access door was nailed shut, and the only way we could get to our hot-tub was by going outside wearing dressing gowns, which hadn't been ideal through the winter, but that tub was such a great way to get warm when it was really cold, that it didn't matter. Unfortunately, we had to get really cold again, getting back into the house by going outside.

It was Ian who did the digging out, as it proved to have no topsoil, and was just very solid, very dry clay, but it would have to be cleared out first, as it was littered with bits of old wire, rubble, old laths – probably from when the previous owner had taken down the bedroom walls and ceilings in what was now our bedroom and library – and would take quite a bit of shifting.

When it came to the mixing, it was both of us. I was OICCM – Officer in Charge of Cake Mixes – and Ian was humper and pourer. I was back to full fitness, and could manage to load the cement mixer, although my spade only managed to deliver half as much as Ian's, so I had to double all the numbers in the recipe.

I must admit that he had done the first small section without any help, but it took so long, and achieved so little, that I took over my old role of Shortly, and he took his of O'Reilly, the Irish builder. I was called Shortly because every time I asked him when he was going to pay me – in the appropriate accent, of course, – he always replied, 'Shortly,' and it stuck.

We had a lot of harmless fun in the heavily Irish voices we used in our banter, and working together in character often had us in stitches of laugher. On the very first occasion these characters had emerged, when laying a patio at our last house in the UK, I had worn a fairly low-cut T-shirt, or at least it was when I downed tools for a little rest. Ian took one look at me and declared in his cod-Irish, 'Sure, I can see your front builder's bottom, Shortly.' I laughed till I cried, and it still makes me smile, writing about it here.

It took four more days of back-breaking work, but we finally finished, and left the last section of our handiwork to dry before having a proper inspection of exactly what we had achieved. When we did, we were horrified at how uneven it was, when Ian had tried his hardest to tamp it down to a level surface when he laid it.

This resulted in an emergency visit from Barney, who had now finished working three days a week for us. He took one look at it, then gave us an old-fashioned look that seemed to say, 'amateurs – what are they like?'

'I can sort that out,' he said. 'I'll even it off with a bit more concrete, and then I'll use some *ragréage*.' We didn't know what that was, but it turned out to be some sort of concrete leveller, and he had saved our bacon again, as we wanted him to tile not just that room, but right through the Jacuzzi room as well. We asked him to give us an approximate figure for labour, and told him we'd get in touch when we had the money, not only for his time, but for the tiles and adhesive as well – grout we could probably afford without too much scrimping and saving – and sent him on his way.

BACK ON THE HAMSTER WHEEL AGAIN

Meanwhile, I had been contemplating a way in which I could supplement our income. At the beginning of this year, new legislation had opened up the market for the small-time self-employed to work, without using the *micro-entreprise* system. It was for a new type of small business for only one person, and they, after registration, would be known *as auto-entrepreneurs*.

I got Ian to register me online, not knowing at the time that a wrongly-pressed key would cause nearly a year's worth of trouble for us, and prepared to go back to teaching music. We flooded the supermarkets with postcards with contact details on them, and sat back waiting for something to happen, which it did, quite soon.

My first call was from a Dutch lady who wanted to learn the violin. She was a retired lady whose English was rather wobbly, and we communicated on the phone in a mixture of French and English. The night before her first lesson, I sat in tears, terrified of not being able to communicate with her, and worried about my current state of expertise, for I had not played this instrument for a long time.

I need not have worried, for she turned out to be a joy to know, and went on to tackle other instruments as well. We settled on a mixture of languages, and I kept a Dutch-English dictionary handy, for when we were lost for words in both languages. Her lessons became rather like a music hall double act, and we would often be convulsed with laughter at some of the things that caused us linguistic problems. She has become a firm friend, and I am truly fond of her.

Shortly afterwards, I had an enquiry from a lady who lived about fifty kilometres away, but was offering me the chance to teach, not only her son the guitar, but to follow on with lessons for the children of one of her acquaintances, one on flute, one on guitar and one on piano. It might be a long drive, but it would certainly be worth the petrol money. Thus my career as a music teacher in France, which was to endure for some years into the future, had begun, with Ian driving me the hundred-kilometre round trip every Monday after school hours.

After that, I had a steady trickle of enquiries which led me to teach quite a few other instruments that I played, including the saxophone and the clarinet and, for a short time, even the viola. I, basically, had a ball, what with changing hats as I changed instruments. It has been a great deal of fun, and I am grateful to all the students who chose me as their teacher.

I had never seen my twenty-five years of teaching as work, not even that as a Greek and English teacher, but rather as play, so I wasn't at all upset at getting back into the rat race, as my rat race was a good deal slower than Ian's had ever been, and was extremely unlikely to cause a heart attack.

THE SMOTHERING COILS OF BUREAUCRACY

Going to the doctor and getting the necessary pills and potions should be easy. At the point when we stopped getting medical coverage from the UK, we presumed that the original *Carte Vitale* (card entitling one to medical coverage from the French government) we had received on registering here as residents would be changed to one that indicated that I was now working, and that a different country was covering our expenses for hospital visits and monthly medication as well as visits to the doctor. We got nothing, but expected they were waiting for our cover to run out from the UK government, and it would be done then.

What actually happened was that, one day in the pharmacy, my card was simply rejected from the machine, and we had to pay for the medication ourselves. This was quite a strain on our finances as we were both on multiple medications. The same thing happened the next month, and the pharmacy, to which we had been very loyal, took up our plight on the telephone but, after forty-five minutes being passed from pillar to post, the poor woman had to admit defeat.

We eventually found out that when Ian registered me as an *auto-entrepreneur*, he had ticked a box that declared I was retired which, in theory, I was, in that I didn't do any paid work any more. What the box wanted to know, however, was whether I was over retirement age, and whether I received any pensions. The organisation that was currently covering us as a retired couple (!) did not cover people who were working, and we would have to get my status changed, and be moved to another organisation, with me providing the cover instead of Ian, who had a pension, albeit a tiny one. I needed to be designated head of the household officially.

It sounds simple, doesn't it? Not here! It took nine months of letters and phone calls and frustrating tangles with apparently impenetrable rules and regulations to achieve this, and all this time, we had had to pay, each month, for our own tablets, pills and potions. Thank God I didn't have to go into hospital during this period, as we later learnt that the amount it had cost the organisation and our top-up private insurance company for my three previous stays there, was in excess of twenty thousand euros!

It took nine months of wrangling before we eventually received our new, correct cards, Ian getting cover from me being the only French taxpayer and, even then, it wasn't over. The new organisation now needed all our *vignettes* before we could have what we had paid out could be paid back to us. What in the name of God were they, we wondered.

We soon found out that every box of medication which had been issued to us had a tiny bar-coded pull-off strip which the pharmacist was supposed to have stuck on our prescription sheet, which lasted for three months, and these tiny self-adhesive strips were what they were after. We would now need to find every box we had emptied going back nine months!!!

We did eventually manage to come across quite a lot of them but the pharmacy provided us with quite a lot, using their back records, from medication issued to people who didn't need their vignettes for anything, which was very kind of them, but I suppose they did it because they had not actually stuck them on to our prescription sheets at the time, as they should have. Then we had to stick them to sheets of paper, send them off and wait … and wait … and wait.

Eventually, we were refunded fifteen hundred euros and were able to hold our new cards in our hands. I remember this time well, and with trepidation, because I am about to change organisations again, and am glad we know how long everything could take, how complicated it is, and how patient we will have to be.

ENTER AN OLD FRIEND

It was about this time that we had a call from an old friend from the UK whom we had not seen for some time, and we immediately asked him to come over to stay, not just to see the house, but so that we could catch up on our friendship. We had not seen him for more than two years; not since he had moved north, and we looked forward to his arrival enthusiastically.

It was great to see him again, and we had a fabulous week, not just showing him the state of our house, but the local area as well, and introducing him to some of our friends, two of whom we saw regularly to play cards, snack and drink wine.

We had met this couple, the Forrests, at Paul and Denise's house one evening and, the weather turning inclement, the four of us had departed early, as we had been sitting outside, and we invited them over to see our place. This was some time ago, now, for the big upstairs had been still in its barn-like state and lacked any form of electricity.

They were eager to have a look, as they had considered buying it themselves, shortly before we did, but had only ever looked at the outside, and they didn't live far away now. They currently had a little bungalow which they were extending, set in thirteen acres of woodland and a lake with its own island.

At our place we did the honours, then opened some wine, and our evening ended considerably later than that of Paul and Denise. We had become immediate friends, and they invited us over to their place, where they were living a bit of the good life, with chickens, quail, and goats as well as their two dogs.

The island bit was enchanting, with Mrs Forrest declaring that she wanted to be buried on it, but the electric gates, the very long drive and the concentration of trees certainly cured me of any jealousy I thought I would feel. Although the bungalow was in a good-sized clearing, the thought of being that far away from the gates – which, being electric, would not work in the event of the many and frequent power cuts – and enclosed by so much woodland, I found it all rather like the start of a Stephen King book, and shuddered at the thought. I was perfectly content with what I had, thank you very much.

We took our visiting friend, Arthur, over to see them and their lifestyle, and we could see that, with other trips out and about, and the growing vegetable garden that we now had, he was getting a very far-away look in his eyes from time to time. It looked ominous, and so it proved to be.

Two days after he went back to the UK, he phoned and asked us if he could come back in a week. As he was self-employed, he didn't need to consult anyone about when he took time off, with the exception of his clients, and they were very easy-going. And so he returned and, by then, we had heard that the French couple opposite had begun to think of selling up, as they had other properties which were, at the moment anyway, rented out.

He went over for a secret viewing with the idea that he might live just opposite us in the future, a circumstance that I don't think his ex-wife would at all have approved of, as we still kept in touch with her, having refused to take sides in their separation, not wanting to lose the friendship of either, so long had we known each other. That wasn't a comfortable thought for us, but we said nothing, and he came back saying that the price was ridiculously high, and the property too small and totally unsuitable.

We did get a look round it ourselves, later, and he was right. It needed too much spent on it, and their price was far too ambitious.

Now, did we know any local estate agents? he wanted to know. Yes, Arthur, we know some of them quite well, we explained, after the two frantic periods of viewing with Kay and Robert, and our own 'pretend' (my arse) viewings, in 2007. We would go into town, find some properties and arrange some viewings for him the very next day, we promised him. Here we go again, I thought.

The next morning, we tootled into town, and went to the agency we were most familiar with. The woman who had worked there when we enquired before and arranged for us an introduction to Mr and Mrs Chandler had left, and in her place was a younger woman who was considerably younger and slimmer. As we began to explain to him what Arthur was looking for, sparks began to fly between the two of them – and she was married.

We were familiar with many properties that were still on the market, because we had seen them before, when Kay and Robert were looking at houses, and I more or less took over and dismissed, out of hand, a lot of old rubbish she was trying to persuade us was habitable. Arthur eventually made his selection, and left her to sort out the appointments.

The next day she picked him up and took him off to look at a few at which she had managed to obtain appointments, but he came back rather down in the mouth. No good? We asked him, and he shook his head in disappointment. 'She has, however, made two appointments for me tomorrow, but you'll have to take me to them. I've already got the keys to one of the places – she trusted me enough to have them overnight – but we've got to return them to the office tomorrow after we've had a look.

At the sight of his disappointed face, we instantly filled a couple of carafes with wine and herded him upstairs to the library, where we put on some soothing music and prepared to look at the sheaf of house details he had brought back with him. It would be good for him to go through why the ones he had rejected were unsuitable, and fun for all of us to go through details she had given him the day before, before he'd got out of the car.

We did have quite a good time, quaffing and pontificating, all the time grateful that his viewings the next day were in the afternoon.

Our first viewing the following day was of what has become a more common type of house over here, even since we arrived – the wooden one. This one had been up for a few years, as proved by the state of the weathering of the timber and, unfortunately, as we discovered quite quickly, already had woodworm. The design was terrible and the order was poor. It was not old, as more solid dwellings go, but it was definitely very tired, and more than Arthur wanted to take on.

The second viewing was of an old stone house which had been used, for some years, as a holiday home, had three inter-connecting rooms and a kitchen on the ground floor and three bedrooms plus a mezzanine and a bathroom on the first floor. Personally, I wasn't over keen, but it had sparked some interest in our friend, as he looked around at what he could do with it. It also had a barn, accessible from the last of the inter-connecting rooms, and a fair bit of land. It certainly sent him into thoughtful mood, but we didn't discuss it much, as we all made an early night of it, after the late one we had had the evening before.

Arthur was very perky the next morning – probably because he was off with his lady estate agent again for some more viewings. Good luck to him. I suddenly realised that I didn't want to see another set of house details for some time to come. I'd finally had enough of poking my nose into other people's lifestyles. It could be very depressing over here, especially when it involved giving up and going back to England, or a divorce – or even both.

He returned that evening in neutral mood. He'd seen nothing that spoke to him, but he had enjoyed the company. Down, Tiger! She's a married woman. We went off upstairs to the library again for some more pontificating, looking at the details of what he'd viewed that day and, after we'd done that, he said he'd really liked the house that was currently a holiday home, and that he'd like to arrange a second viewing.

That was easy to arrange the next morning, as the agent

had the keys between owner's visits, so off we went again that afternoon, having picked up the keys on our way through. Arthur spent a lot of time walking around muttering to himself, occasionally making a note on the details, of ideas he'd just had, and we left him to it. If he liked it, it was him who would be living in it, and nothing to do with us.

He was very quiet in the car back, only becoming a bit more lively when he dropped the keys into the office. That evening, he was still up to sinking a few glasses upstairs, but he was very thoughtful. 'Penny for them,' I eventually prompted him, and he reminded us that he still hadn't sold his mother's house, which would fund this purchase.

'You'll just have to have a word with Mata Hari, about how anxious they are to sell,' I said.

'And I could put my flat on the market,' he suddenly crowed. 'Only one of the properties would have to sell, to fund me moving over here.' He had a plan now, and spoke to the agent the next morning, discovering that the owner was in no particular hurry to sell, provided he had a firm offer.

That evening, Arthur made one, having obtained the apple of his eye's mobile number. She immediately contacted the owner who agreed the price, which was considerably lower than what they were asking, and it had been agreed that the house wouldn't be actively marketed any more. That was an evening of real celebration, and he kept saying, 'I've bought a house in France! I've actually bought a house in France.'

There's many a slip 'twixt cup and lip, and he hadn't actually bought it. There were some trials to come before that became a reality, and he moved, lock stock and barrel, to a village not too far from us, but at least one friend wanted to live near us.

From that time forward, he would come out about every two or three weeks to have another look and do some measuring of what was to be his new kingdom. This proved very helpful to us, while we were in a covered-in-paint phase, leaving Ian to get on with one room while I did the reachable part of another, with Arthur doing all the bits that involved a ladder, so our progress went on at a great pace during these interludes.

Eventually he had an acceptable offer for his late mother's house, and began to try to establish a completion date, and plan the move of all his worldly goods. We, of course, gave him Kynaston's number, as his prices are very keen, and he'd need every centime to get his new abode up to snuff.

He was, however, getting some pressure now from the owners of the house over here, to fix a date for the purchase of their holiday home, and we stepped in to help him out, using our emergency fund, as he was having trouble with the buyers of his mother's house. It was only supposed to be for about six weeks, but it turned into six months, although it did have a happy ending.

He came over again just before the completion of his purchase, as the soon-to-be previous owners had decided to have a house sale of all the contents, and both he and we moseyed around to see if there was anything we fancied ourselves. There were a few things, but most of the stuff had ridiculous price tags on it, and the estate agent who had sold it and was responsible for this part of the procedure as well, had no discretion about the set prices.

I had fallen in love with a huge oak sideboard that was currently in the kitchen, but they wanted two hundred and fifty euros for it, and we simply didn't have that sort of money in those days, so I said a fond farewell to it on the last day of the sale. Arthur bought very little, too, as he had all his own stuff, and we knew a place where he could pick up second-hand furniture for very reasonable prices – most unusual for France – and he very sensibly decided to wait.

EVEN MORE CATS

A while after he went back to England this time, we heard from our friends Gerhard and Ellen that Mr Smelly's cats had produced kittens again, and that he intended to drown them. 'Telephone him now, and we'll take what we can,' I cried, much to Ian's disgust. She was the only one of the four of us who could do this, as she spoke not only German, French, and English, but could understand the weird patois that he spoke, and could also answer in the same impenetrable – to us – lingo.

I then phoned Arthur and asked him if he intended to have any cats when he was living here, and he said he wouldn't mind a couple. Great! Ellen let us know when we could go to have a look, and, a few days later, we set off, at least prepared in advance from our previous visits, for the Great Stink.

Two of his cats had produced this time to his knowledge but, in between Ellen speaking to him and our visit, one of his cats who was a bit more canny than the others, had sneaked off into the woods, given birth there, and not brought her offspring back to the house until their eyes were open. She'd obviously worked out that if he found them when they were new-born, she'd lose them, whereas, if she brought them back a little older (and much, much cuter) he wouldn't have the heart to do away with them.

When we arrived, he had one cat with a litter of three blacks and two that showed signs of having some Siamese heritage. The second cat had two blacks (one much bigger than his two litter mates, and one that wouldn't survive) and a pale, slightly oriental one. The sneaky cat had a couple of slightly older kittens which had very finely striped tabby coats with no white at all.

Arthur had given us carte blanche to choose whichever cats we thought fit for him, but we had first choice.

Looking at the number we had to choose from, knowing we had agreed we would only choose two and Arthur wanted the same number, we went completely off plan, and broke all the rules.

We chose one of the lightning-pawed tabbies, one of the blacks from the second mother, and the Siamese-like one from the same litter. A couple of days later, we found we had both been haunted by a long-haired Siamese type who was the surviving weak one from the second mother, which always looked a complete mess, covered in wee from the floor, her rear end permanently poo-smattered. Her fur was a complete mess, and she was much smaller than the others. She was not in the least attractive, but had seemed to plead with us with her eyes when we had last seen her. Without a lot of love and care, we didn't think she would live.

We had both been quietly thinking about this bedraggled little scrap, wondering what the old man would do with her once the other had gone and, almost simultaneously, asked each other if we ought to go back and say we'd take her as well. Talk about a walk-over. We did so, and ear-marked three blacks and a Siamese type for Arthur. I was adamant that he wouldn't mind if we reserved four for him. If we took four as well, that only left one, which Mr Smelly had said a friend would take. Phew! We'd saved this lot, but it wasn't something we could do on a regular basis.

Arthur was very compliant, once I had explained to him what would probably happen to the kittens if we didn't find takers for them and, although he'd never had a cat before, said he'd give it a go, with a baptism of fire, by having four. He didn't even mind having three blacks, because they were easy to distinguish from the lengths of their fur, and was really looking forward to this new experience.

I, of course, being a girl, immediately set about

deciding on names for them. The little tabby darling ran like the wind, so we decided to call him Button after the Formula 1 driver, Jenson Button. The long-haired black one, who was the giant of the second litter, we decided, would have Clarkson as a suitable moniker. The little Siamese type had a very serious look of deep thought on his face and, after watching a television detective programme, we named him after one of the main characters, Brian.

The runty, long-haired, messy oriental type had us stumped, however, until it crept into the conversation, one evening on the phone, that Arthur's baby name was Boo, and so she became Boo, in homage to his babyhood. The only thing I knew about my early life is a frequently told story about how my father was always moaning, 'Does that baby never sleep?' Not quite the name for a kitten, is it? It doesn't have a ring to it, like Boo.

Arthur decided that he would call his after some of his favourite marionette figures and, thus, the Siamese girl became Lady Penelope – Penny-poos after a while, as she, like Boo, suffered from dribbly bum – Troy Tempest, shortened to TT, Virgil, shortened to Verge, and Scotty. He never has grown up.

And so the scene was set to have one of our old friends join us on our adventure, and eight new cats to enter our lives. We also had plans to push ahead with renovating the part of the barn that we had concreted, and to put in an above-ground pool the same size as the one we had had in England. That would take an awful lot of concrete for the base, and some digging out, as no ground, no matter how flat it looks, always has humps and bumps and sloping bits, that the brain somehow edits out when looking at the piece of land.

There were also two windows to fit in the barn, as there were two openings with nothing at all to stop intruders, and two that needed replacing as they were so old and rotten. We still had the barn roof to be re-laid, the old lime mortar to be taken off the walls of the house and replaced, the repair of the stonework round the windows and doors, and the coigne stones, and doors to have made for two of the large openings into the huge barn structure.

We also needed new shutters made for both the house and barn, and had four windows to be replaced by double-glazing, three of them hand-made for the north-facing bedrooms, because of the curvy nature of the frames, as we weren't allowed to alter anything about the outside of the house apart from maintenance, because of the presence of the historic church opposite. We needed new gates, front and back, and a drive dug-out and laid to stop the passage through the property from becoming like the Somme in the wet months.

We also needed to replace one of the windows (currently single-glazed), and the en-suite bathroom window also needed double glazing. Add to this that the stones in the dining room needed to be done in *pierre apparent* (which is a fancy form of pointing), and the *séjour* needed a new floor and ceiling. There was also the outside woodwork, which was in a terrible state, we needed three new log burners of the more efficient (and working) variety installed, with flues that complied with current French law …

The list could go on and on. So far, we had only scratched the surface of what was needed to turn this house into the one I saw in my mind's eye, when we first saw it. As I write this now, it is February 2014. Although a lot happened between the end of this book and now, we are still nowhere near finished. There's plenty of stuff still to write about and about which to laugh – when we look back on it. At the time, some things simply aren't funny because they seem so serious but, with the buffer of time, they become our favourite anecdotes, which we can tell with a wry smile to anyone who will take the time to listen.

I can't wait to start remembering some of the disasters and pickles we got ourselves into. So far, this adventure has been a blast, with twists and turns in our fortunes that would put a rollercoaster to shame.

Before I sign off, though, I want to say a word about the weather – always an English obsession. Having seen the full round of the seasons, I can conclude that the climate here is the climate I remember as a child in England – no doubt through the rose-tinted spectacles of memory.

Spring comes surprisingly early, and it is possible to get tanned in February. The summer is very long, not usually ending until the middle of October. Autumn is filled with colour from the trees, under a sky as blue as a speedwell. Winters are bitingly cold but bright, with amazingly jewelled frosts, with the occasional fall of snow which, once the sky has cleared again, stays for days rather than hours, covering the landscape in a glorious Christmas cake confection of white.

Here, the weather is weather, and the warming up of the rain is not the only sign of summer coming. We are not enclosed in a cloudy dome of greyness, and it gladdens the heart to see such brightness and contrast. When we first found this place, I thought it was the house in which I was going to die. While I am not completely convinced of this any more, there being so many other adventures to have before I go off on the greatest adventure of them all, I am happy and content, and look forward to our home looking the way I saw it in my mind's eye when we first moved here. It is slowly getting there.

Until the next time – au revoir!

THE END

Other titles
by
Andrea Frazer

For more information about

Andrea Frazer

please visit

Amazon author page

Printed in Great Britain
by Amazon